BONNYBRIDGE LIBRARY
BRIDGE STREET
BONNYBRIDGE
STIRLINGSHIRE FK4 1AD
TEL. 503295

Falkirk Council Library Services

This book is due for return on or before the last date indicated on the label. Renewals may be obtained on application.

Bo'ness 01506 778520	Falkirk 503605	Grangemouth 504690
Bonnybridge 503295	Mobile 506800	Larbert 503590
Denny 504242		Slamannan 851373

23 OCT 2012   08 JAN 2015

23 AUG 2010   27 SEP 2013   16 MAR 2015

08 SEP 2010   22 OCT 2013   30 APR 2015

−3 SEP 2015

22 OCT 2010

26 MAY 2014   11 FEB 2016

22 OCT 2010   03 JAN 2014

25 JUN 2011   07 JUL 2014

25 NOV 2011

Serial Killers:
The World's
Most Evil

Serial Killers: The World's Most Evil

NIGEL BLUNDELL

First published in Great Britain in 2010 by
WHARNCLIFFE TRUE CRIME
An imprint of
Pen & Sword Books Ltd
47 Church Street
Barnsley
South Yorkshire
S70 2AS

ISBN 978-1-84563-118-5

The right c | **Falkirk Council** | his work has
been ass(| | esigns and

| **BB** | |

| **Askews** | |

All rights re: | | r transmitted
in any | 364.1523 | £19.99 | icluding
photocopyin | | rieval system,

Typeset by Concept, Huddersfield, West Yorkshire
Printed and bound by the MPG Books Group in the UK

Pen & Sword Books Ltd incorporates the imprints of Pen & Sword Aviation,
Pen & Sword Maritime, Pen & Sword Military, Wharncliffe Local History,
Pen & Sword Select, Pen & Sword Military Classics, Leo Cooper,
Remember When, Seaforth Publishing and Frontline Publishing.

For a complete list of Pen & Sword titles please contact
PEN & SWORD BOOKS LIMITED
47 Church Street, Barnsley, South Yorkshire, S70 2AS, England
E-mail: enquiries@pen-and-sword.co.uk
Website: www.pen-and-sword.co.uk

Contents

Foreword

By Dr Michael Stone, world renowned forensic psychiatrist

We all have a fascination with evil. Think of evil as a large dark-watered lake where many an author has gone fishing, aiming to catch the 'ten most evil people ever' or the 'ten most evil people now living' ... The list is getting pretty long. Most of these authors get the wartime evildoers (the big fish, like Hitler and Saddam Hussein and Caligula) mixed in with the peacetime evildoers (the littler, but still impressive, fish like Jack the Ripper or Charles Manson).

If we're to grasp evil in some meaningful way, we need to keep the wartime folk separate from the peacetime folk. Their psychology and their backgrounds are often quite different. The men and women who do evil deeds in peacetime, and who do so repetitively, are not answering to some political doctrine.

But even the peacetime folk are not all cut from the same cloth. Some have done one extraordinarily wicked act and have later repented; others are violent psychopaths with brains programmed to do evil crimes from sunup till sundown, devoid of any redeeming, human qualities. Often they are devoted to the prolonged torture of their victims.

Serial slayers at this farthest end of the scale, like Ian Brady and Rose and Fred West, have certain things about them that are remarkably different from most other killers. For a start, those committing serial sexual homicide tend to have extreme sexual demands – what we call hyper-sexuality. And they almost invariably have one or more peculiar sexual outlets. They may have abnormal obsessions like voyeurism or exhibitionism or become sexually aroused by the pain of their victims. Or they may want to bind them, practise cannibalism or necrophilia.

If you see even one murder where a woman is raped and strangled and where the crime is them staged – the body is dumped somewhere in a very embarrassing or insulting position, perhaps with legs spread apart – you know you are dealing with a vicious killer who probably gets off on that sort of thing. He is very likely to have done it before to somebody else or is about to embark on a career of doing it again.

At the time he's only struck once, he's a serial killer manqué – but you know that there will be a second or a third or more. The FBI used three murders to identity someone as a serial killer. For me, one or two will do. For it is often possible to tell from a first crime whether that person's character is likely to turn the perpetrator into a repeat killer. I believe that if you commit a certain kind of vicious crime and you have certain personality characteristics, such as you are identified as a psychopath, then you're too dangerous to be released. And we should incarcerate that person for as long as it takes until we can really satisfy ourselves that the dangerousness has passed. And if it hasn't, then that person should remain inside. The factors can be so great that the idea of releasing anyone like that is ridiculous.

These are the levels of criminality that merit the title *The World's Most Evil*. And author Nigel Blundell has got it right. Just as in his recent book *Crafty Crooks & ConMen*, where he serves us up a rich menu of swindlers and fraudsters (alas, the book came to press a few months before the exploits of Bernie Madoff came to light, but Bernie Cornfeld is there, along with the televangelists Jimmy Swaggart and Jim Bakker), Blundell now serves up an authentic list of truly irredeemable, evil killers, all of whom were active within the past fifty years, and almost all of whom were demonic practitioners of torture.

Some of the names are so well-known as to have achieved iconic status – like Belgium's Marc Dutroux and Fred and Rosemary West in the UK. Others are less well-known but had subjected their victims to even more gruesome and horrifying tortures – like Lawrence Bittaker and David Parker Ray and Leonard Lake, all from the American West, but worse than any cowboy ever dreamed of being.

Nigel Blundell has managed to put together an anthology of evil men and women who actually did – and did repeatedly – crimes beyond what you ever imagined doing to your worst enemy. That is what evil is all about. That is why Blundell's book goes to the head of the list. Stories to make you cringe. Stories you can't put down.

Michael H. Stone, MD

Introduction

If, as with any other human trait, there are degrees of evil, then at the bottom of the pit of depravity must be those murderers we label 'serial killers'. That has been the justifiable view of civilised society through the ages. However, in recent years, criminologists have categorised an even deeper level of wickedness. For there are those among the ranks of serial killers whose sick psyche and deeds of degeneracy put them in a class of their own – at the very bottom of the barrel. This book is about them.

On an internationally acknowledged 'Scale of Evil', the characters catalogued in the following pages are the world's very worst murderers. The qualification for being labelled a serial killer is, according to America's Federal Bureau of Investigation, a body count of three separate slayings. The qualifications for entry to this book's list of the vilest criminals of all time are somewhat narrower – in short, they must have a propensity for sadism, torture and murder without a shred of remorse.

Using expert evidence, *Serial Killers: The World's Most Evil* looks behind the shocking headlines and delves into the minds of these monsters. What drives them to crime? What turns seemingly ordinary members of society into sick slayers? How do they self-justify their heinous deeds? And, quite simply, how have they so often got away with murder?

To attempt to answer these questions, the author has drawn on the experience of a man who probably knows more about 'pure evil' than anyone else on earth. He is world-renowned forensic psychiatrist Dr Michael Stone MD, who has spent thirty years delving into the darkest recesses of the minds of these monsters. Dr Stone began studying serial killers in 1987 when he first started collating his 'Scale of Evil' to rank and measure the depravity of some of the world's most reviled criminals. He wanted to find out what drives seemingly normal men and women to such horrific crimes – and discover whether it is possible to prevent people committing psychopathic acts.

After profiling hundreds of the most evil minds of all time, he came up with the key genetic, environmental and neurological factors that may drive a person to kill. And he was able to measure those who are truly evil, as opposed to those who commit evil acts.

Over several meetings with Dr Stone, the soft-spoken American scientist explained how the grading of perpetrators of violent crime is made possible – and how it can help prevent further acts of homicide. He has also expounded on his theories in a fascinating volume, *The Anatomy of Evil* (Prometheus Books, 2009), which is 'must reading' for anyone interested in this subject.

Michael Stone MD, who is a professor of clinical psychiatry at Columbia University's College of Physicians and Surgeons, has written several previous books and is the host of television series such as Discovery Channel's *Most Evil*. From his research of more than 600 biographies of murderers, he has developed his scale – officially labelled the 'Gradations of Evil' – with twenty-two levels stretching from 'justified homicide' (not evil at all) to 'jealousy murder' (Level 2) all the way up to 'murder after prolonged torture' (Level 22).

While not following Dr Stone's own American-oriented lists precisely, the author has attempted to follow his overall guidelines. All of the killers included in this book have been studied by Dr Stone. Most of them are at the top of his 'Scale of Evil'. Perhaps unexpectedly within a book on the very worst serial killers, some of the body counts of these murderers are relatively low. Theresa Knorr killed 'only' two – but they were her own children and they died in a manner that puts her at the pinnacle of evil. Sante Kimes and son Kenny did not notch up a high murder count – at least officially – yet the calculating nature of their crimes also categorises them as 'most evil'.

Other entrants in this catalogue of psychopathic killers are men who committed crimes so monstrous that they almost defy belief, yet to their neighbours and work colleagues seemed quite normal. Dennis Rader was a respected pillar of society yet set out on nightly killing sprees. David Parker Ray was just an 'average working guy' but had a torture chamber in his backyard. John Wayne Gacy was a kids' entertainer but his slaying spree earned him the media tag 'Killer Clown'.

Then there are criminal partnerships whose wickedness must have seemed blatantly obvious at the time, yet who for too long remained undetected. Fred and Rose West raised a large extended family who they violently abused and murdered. Ian Brady and Myra Hindley sickeningly captured the screams of a tortured child on tape and used it as an aphrodisiac. Leonard Lake and his partner in crime Charles Ng subjected women to intense prolonged torture to make snuff movies.

These and the other murderers in this book are examples of those who sank to the darkest depths of depravity. The aim of *Serial Killers: The World's Most Evil* is to discover the clues as to what made them such monsters. The book will also hopefully demonstrate that there are fiends in our midst who are beyond redemption and who should be locked up without hope of remission. The sadness, as criminologists like Dr Stone have pointed out, is that we so seldom detect the danger signs in time to save their victims' lives. Yet those signals are often clear to see – as the following pages will dramatically reveal.

CHAPTER 1

David Parker Ray

Is this man the most evil serial killer of modern times?

The monster named 'officially' as the most evil killer in recent history has never been convicted of murder. He is David Parker Ray, who was charged with kidnapping, raping and torturing women in and around a small American town with the strange name of Truth or Consequences.

Ray drugged his victims to erase their memories and kept them chained up in a horrifying backyard torture chamber which he referred to as 'Satan's Den' or 'The Toy Box'. But because this vile but intelligent man successfully hid the bodies of as many as sixty victims, he literally got away with murder. He was never convicted of the ultimate crime – nor was his daughter, who helped him procure his victims, or his girlfriend who assisted him. Ray himself escaped a lengthy term in prison – by dying in 2002 of heart failure only eight months into his sentence.

David Parker Ray's forty-year reign of terror had ended three years earlier when one of his would-be victims escaped. Dark-haired beauty Cynthia Vigil ran screaming through the streets of Elephant Butte, New Mexico, on 22 March 1999, naked, with a metal dog collar around her neck and trailing a chain. Sobbing, almost incoherently, 21-year-old Cynthia claimed she had been held captive for three days and subjected to a terrifying ordeal of rape and torture. She named her kidnapper as 59-year-old David Parker Ray, a loner with four failed marriages, who lived on the borders of Elephant Butte Lake State Park, where he worked for the park authorities and as a mechanic.

Police arrested Ray and searched his home, where they found evidence of a struggle in his living room which supported

Cynthia's claims. But a greater shock was in store when officers opened a white trailer parked in his backyard and discovered a horrifying torture chamber. The centrepiece of the room was a gynaecological chair fitted with straps, surrounded by an array of torture instruments and twisted sex toys. This was Ray's 'Toy Box' or 'Satan's Den', as he named it.

There seemed little doubt that Cynthia Vigil's story of sexual degradation was true. 'She was his sex slave when they entered this trailer,' said Norman Rhoades of the state police. 'The first thing my eyes focussed on was the black chair – a gynaeco-logical chair. A feeling of sickness came over me. Everything around me – sadistic pictures on the walls, straps and chains, a bar he'd labelled "ankle stretcher", sex toys attached to power drills, dildos with nails embedded in them – everything in that trailer denoted pain and destruction. Once he'd drugged them, he could get a woman in any position he wanted. They were his sex slaves.'

Fellow officer Captain Rich Libicer said: 'Trinkets hidden in the room raised the likelihood that other women had suffered a similar fate. It was pretty clear that there were going to be more victims. Once that Pandora's Box was opened, I never doubted that we'd found a serial killer.'

The policemen found two fixed video cameras and a tape containing footage of another of Ray's victims strapped to the chair. The woman, apparently drugged or unconscious, could only be identified by an unusual tattoo on her leg. When the tattoo was shown in the press and on TV, a woman came forward to identify herself. She was 25-year-old Kelly Van Cleave, then living in Colorado, but previously a child minder and friend of Ray's 34-year-old daughter, Glenda Jean, known as 'Jessy'.

Kelly had been drugged and chained inside the 'Toy Box' as Ray's tortured sex slave. Astonishingly, she had no memory of being abducted or held captive – but said she had been tor-mented by nightmares of being tied down and tortured. 'My nightmares were about being tied to a table, handcuffed, re-strained with tape,' she later recalled. 'But when the FBI called, then I knew they weren't just dreams.'

Under police questioning, Kelly found some of her memories returning. It was clear that she had been drugged to prevent her from remembering the trauma. The use of sedatives also explained why more women had not come forward.

More chilling evidence soon emerged – a tape recording in which Ray explained to his victims what he was about to do to them. Coolly but cruelly, he told them: 'You'll be (he explains the forms of sexual abuse) thoroughly and repeatedly. You'll be drugged up real heavy with Phenobarbital and Sodium Pentothal (to numb pain and induce amnesia). You're not going to remember a f****** thing about this little adventure.' He added that he had 'no qualms about slitting your throat' because 'you're a piece of meat to me'.

On the tape, Ray claimed to have abducted over thirty-seven women, leading police to believe that many of them were dead. A massive search of the area and the surrounding desert was conducted, including Elephant Butte Lake, 200 yards deep, in the state park where Ray was warden and had a sailing boat. Not a single body was found, however, and prosecutors decided a murder charge was impossible.

'The fact that we couldn't prosecute him for murder made it all the more important that we successfully prosecute him for the rape, torture and kidnapping,' said the chief prosecutor, Deputy District Attorney Jim Yontz.

Yet the case against Ray rested on two potentially unreliable witnesses. Cynthia Vigil was a heroin-addicted prostitute, while Kelly Van Cleave had only partial memories of her experience. Moreover, at Ray's trial in July 2000, the judge ruled that the tape recording of Ray was inadmissible. To the shock and horror of his surviving victims, the trial ended in a hung jury, and it looked as if the monster would walk free.

However, at a retrial nine months later, another judge allowed the jury to hear the horrific tape. Said Kelly Van Cleave: 'The voice sent shivers down me. It cut through the air like a knife.'

Once again, everything rested on Kelly's evidence. Unless her testimony was believed by every jury member, the charges against Parker Ray could be dropped. As she later recalled: 'I was vulnerable. I was scared. But I was angry that he got away with the first one. Was he going to get away with the second one?'

Kelly bravely relived her courtroom ordeal for a 2008 TV documentary, in which she revealed her feelings for the first time. She said: 'It's very difficult to tell people you don't know intimate things, sexual things about your life. I think it was harder the second time than it was the first time, because I had already been there. I already had to tell my story to thousands of people I didn't know. And that first jury didn't believe me. At the end of the case, I was sweating. I didn't know what the jury were going to say. I had no idea. But we got "Guilty". And then we partied.'

By the time the unanimous verdict was announced, following a week-long trial on 16 April 2001, David Parker Ray was suspected of killing as many as sixty women. But the numerous charges on which he was convicted did not include any of murder. The offences all involved his crimes against Kelly Van Cleave in July 1996. He later pleaded guilty to charges involving the abduction and sexual torture of two other victims, the 1999 attack on Cynthia Vigil, from Albuquerque, New Mexico, and an assault on the late Angie Montano, of Truth or Consequences.

His defence attorney, Lee McMillan, unsuccessfully argued for withdrawal of Ray's plea on the grounds that his client was incompetent to make informed decisions in prison while under the influence of numerous medications. But Judge Kevin Sweazea ruled that Ray had been alert, responsive, conversant and able to assist in his own defence.

McMillan also pleaded that the term 'paraphilia' (psychosexual disorder) applied to Ray did not do justice to the disease his client had suffered. He argued that Ray, 61, had 'successfully resisted' his disease for almost fifty years and had made efforts to reform himself while in protective custody.

But Mary Ellen O'Toole, an FBI agent expert in sexual sadism, testified that paraphilia was precisely Ray's condition, that he was a 'criminal sexual sadist' of the most dangerous sort, that there was no known therapy for his paraphilia and that its corresponding behaviour could be stopped only by incarceration.

McMillan was equally unsuccessful in his attempt to have Ray's sentence reduced to 173 years suspended, with only ten years actual prison time, which he said was in itself a 'death sentence'. But the lawyer later conceded that his efforts were 'like rearranging deck chairs on the Titanic'.

Before his sentencing, New Mexico's Attorney General, Patricia Madrid, pleaded with the court to impose the maximum penalty, saying the community could not risk any chance of his freedom. She said Ray's plans and his illustrated manual made it clear that he would capture and torture again. He had reduced his victims to abject terror and had thought of them not as human beings but as 'packages'. His behaviour was 'worse than that of any animal'.

Ray's victims were also able to make their statements before the judge pronounced sentence. Kelly Van Cleave, who had earlier been crying and holding hands with Cynthia Vigil in the courtroom, said she wanted Ray to live a long life and to suffer in prison. She said the sick pervert would find no friends in prison and she hoped he would be controlled and used in the same manner as his victims.

Angie Montano's mother, Loretta Romero, said she was in court for her late daughter and her two young sons, whose lives Ray had wrecked. She told how her daughter had lost 'all respect, lost her smile, lost everything' because of Ray. Remarkably, Mrs Romero said she felt sorrow for Ray and forgave him – and was certain her dead daughter would have felt the same way. But, said the anguished mother, 'I can never forget'.

Less forgiving was Cynthia Vigil and her grandmother, who both addressed the court. Cynthia said that no punishment could ever equal the agony she had suffered. In tears, she said she was afraid of the dark and of going out alone, and was perpetually terrified of being tied down and rendered helpless. She hoped Ray would spend the rest of his life in prison and suffer as she had. Turning to Ray, she added: 'I bear scars outside and inside that will never heal.'

Cynthia's grandmother, Mrs Bertha Vigil, told the court her granddaughter had nightmares every night and that Ray had ruined not only her life but her whole family's. Addressing Ray, she called him 'a poor excuse for a human being' and asked him how he would like it if she did to his daughter what he had done to Cynthia. Finally, she said she prayed Ray would suffer every day for the rest of his life, adding: 'Satan has a place for you. I hope you burn in hell forever.'

Summing up, prosecutor Jim Yontz praised the courage of Cynthia and Kelly for their courage in coming to court to relive their horrific experiences. He warned the judge that if Ray was ever released, he would offend before he even got home. 'This monster should never be allowed to walk the streets again,' Yontz said. 'There should be no light at the end of the tunnel and he should realise that a cell will be his home for the rest of his life and that he will leave only in a box.'

While the court listened to these emotional appeals in silent awe, David Parker Ray appeared to be in the best of spirits. He was unmoved when his victims wept while giving their statements.

Acknowledging the presence of his daughter Jessy, who sat in court alongside spectators and press, Ray claimed that he had entered into a plea bargain only for the purpose of obtaining her release from prison on charges of being an accomplice in the abduction of Kelly Van Cleave.

Seeking sympathy, the monster complained he had lost everything: his home, his belongings, his health. But during his two and a half years in confinement, he had had time to reflect, read his Bible and 'get right with God'. He was sorry but could not change the past and had now put his life in the hands of the Almighty.

Showing defiance towards Judge Sweazea, Ray accused him of moving the trial to a venue convenient to the judge's home. By contrast, he praised the original trial judge, Neil Mertz, who had moved the hearing from a local court. That first trial, of course, had resulted in a hung jury.

Predictably, Judge Sweazea was less than swayed. Having heard the testimony of Kelly Van Cleave and Cynthia Vigil, he said he could only imagine the horrors they had suffered. He indicated that the possibility of rehabilitation would not be a consideration in Ray's case. The prime concern would be 'incapacitation'.

For his crimes against Kelly Van Cleave, David Parker Ray was sentenced to nine years for kidnapping, three years for conspiracy to commit kidnapping, eighteen years for each of six counts of criminal sexual penetration, eighteen months for criminal sexual contact, and eighteen months for conspiracy to commit criminal sexual contact.

For his crimes against Cynthia Vigil, Sweazea sentenced Ray to eighteen years for kidnapping, nine years for criminal sexual penetration and nine years for conspiracy to commit kidnapping.

Finding Ray's planning and preparation and the horrific nature of his crimes sufficient to constitute aggravation, the judge imposed an additional one third of the total of the forgoing sentences. All sentences were to be served consecutively – making a total of 224 years, less two and a half years time already served.

Ray's punitive sentence of more than two centuries was in contrast to the course of justice in the case of the other shadowy characters in this horrific case.

Cynthia Hendy, Ray's live-in girlfriend, known to the victims as 'mistress', confessed to being an accessory in the three kidnappings. She supplied testimony against Ray for a reduced sentence of thirty-six years' jail after having the fourteen charges against her cut to just five.

A drifter named Dennis Roy Yancy, described in court as Ray's 'disciple', confessed to strangling to death another kidnap victim, 22-year-old Marie Parker, while Ray took photos. Her body was never found. After a plea deal, he was sentenced to twenty years in prison.

Ray's daughter Jessy was convicted of helping her father kidnap and torture Kelly Van Cleave, yet she was released from custody with five years' probation under a deal with prosecutors conditional upon her father giving up his right to appeal. The deal caused some predictable dismay. Jessy Ray had faced 150 years in prison before multiple counts of 'criminal sexual penetration' and other charges were dropped. But sympathetic observers have since described her not as a fellow monster but as 'a victim'.

The extraordinary background to her involvement in the crimes came to light after her father's arrest when it was revealed that Jessy had reported some of his perversions to the FBI at least thirteen years earlier. David Parker Ray's prosecutor, Deputy District Attorney Jim Yontz, said: 'Jessy Ray actually reported to the FBI her father's activities in 1986. The case of the alleged sexual abuse and slavery of young women and girls was investigated by the FBI in 1986 and 1987 and closed because of insufficient evidence and because they found no victim.'

There was one further instance in this horrific case of justice not being seen to be done. Eight months after David Parker Ray began his jail sentence of 224 years, the monster again cheated justice – by dying, on 28 May 2002, having been locked up for a total of only three years.

Kelly Van Cleave spoke out in anger about his peaceful passing, saying: 'I wish he wouldn't have died. He could have told us what happened to all those other girls, so those other families could have some closure. And I wanted to ask him, Why me? Why pick me? And then, why didn't you kill me?

'My life has gone because of what he did to me. Now I don't go anywhere, don't trust anyone. I miss the old me. I used to be wild, sassy, crazy, scared of nothing. I'd do just about anything to get the old me back.'

David Parker Ray's forty-year reign of terror has earned him the title of 'the world's most evil' in a study by Dr Michael Stone, America's top forensic psychiatrist. Dr Stone (as explained at the start of this book) is the expert who has spent a lifetime delving into the minds of serial killers to devise a 'Scale of Evil', which is used as a sentencing guide by courts in the United States of America and elsewhere. He says: 'Those at the top of the scale are there because they subjected their victims to the most prolonged torture in the most diabolical and physically and psychologically agonising way, with the total absence of remorse and the greatest glee. But David Parker Ray is the "worst of the worst". My Scale of Evil goes from 1 to 22 – but if I had to do it all over, I'd put David Parker Ray in a special Category 23.

'He was a game warden, looked like a nice guy, had married several times and had a daughter – whom he actually enlisted to help him in his crimes. But he had a double life, converting a trailer behind his house into a torture chamber with pulleys, ropes and all kinds of devices.

'He'd drug his victims, often prostitutes, in bars and he'd take them to his place where they would be helplessly tied up. He'd stretch their legs on a rack and insert dildos with nails into their orifices. But before the torture started in earnest, he had a very lengthy fifteen-page single-spaced "manifesto", as he called it, which he had dictated on tape. He'd play the tape, telling the victims what they were about to suffer and how much he didn't give a damn about what happened to them. And then the torture would begin . . . for day, weeks, we don't know how long.

'In my estimation, David Parker Ray is absolutely the worst. I'd have created an extra category in the Scale of Evil just for him – and if he had ever been brought to the execution chamber, I'd have happily pushed the button myself.'

CHAPTER 2

Fred & Rosemary West

'House of Horrors' where children were tortured to death

A notorious murder site always presents a problem. It attracts attention from sick and warped minds and often becomes a regular tourist haunt. It can never resume life as an ordinary family home. It was for these reasons that Gloucester City Council demolished 25 Cromwell Street in October 1996 and turned it into a landscaped footpath. They had every last brick crushed so that nothing remained and no souvenirs could be taken of the 'House of Horrors'. The home of Fred and Rosemary West for over two decades, 25 Cromwell Street had been the scene of such cruelty, torture and ultimately murder – and the final resting place for at least nine of Fred and Rosemary's victims. Its role in history ended on 24 February 1994, when a warrant was obtained to search the house and gardens, leading the police to their grisly discovery of nine mutilated bodies buried in the cellar and under the patio.

Frederick West was born on 29 September 1941. He was his mother's favourite out of his three sisters and two younger brothers and there were rumours that she seduced him when he was just 12 years old. His father, Walter West, was a farm labourer on a Gloucestershire farm. He treated his children as sexual playthings and incest was a way of life for the young Frederick, who adopted the same appetites as his parents, believing it to be natural to behave in this manner. Indeed, when arrested in 1961 for child abuse and impregnating a 13-year-old girl, he seemed completely unfazed, commenting: 'Doesn't everyone do it?' The case never went to trial as the terrified young girl refused to go to court to give evidence. However, Fred's mother, Daisy, rejected him after this scandal and he was sent to live with Aunt Violet in Much Marcle, Herefordshire, on the Welsh Borders.

On 17 November 1962, Fred married Rena Costello. Rena (her real name was Catherine) was five months pregnant at the time by another lover but Fred gave his name to baby Charmaine at her birth. He and Rena soon had their own child, Anne-Marie, and a friend of Rena's, Ann McFall, moved in to help with the childcare.

The Wests' marriage soon ran into trouble. Fred badgered Rena into taking part in sadistic sex games, which she loathed. Ann had become infatuated with Fred and willingly enacted his sexual fantasies, so Rena moved out, returning to Scotland and leaving her children with Fred and Ann. It wasn't long before Ann was pregnant with Fred's baby and continuously urged him to divorce Rena. Instead, he murdered Ann, removing her fingers and toes, a mutilation which was later to become his trademark, and burying her in 'Fingerpost Field', near Much Marcle, along with the body of her unborn baby.

Fred met Rosemary in 1969; she was just 15 years old and already dabbling in prostitution. She lived with her mother and two younger brothers in Cheltenham, having escaped from her violent and incestuous father, William Letts. Fred was 27 and instantly attracted to the busty teenager. They started going steady and within a very short time, Rose had moved in with him, taking on the role of surrogate mother to Charmaine and Anne-Marie.

In October 1970, she gave birth to her own daughter, Heather, rumoured to be the incestuous child of William Letts, with whom Rose had renewed contact after becoming intimate with Fred West. It is said that she had sex with her father, with West's consent, even after their marriage in 1972.

Poor little Charmaine had a tortuous childhood with Fred and Rose. She was abused by the couple and subjected to regular beatings. Witnesses during Rose's trial told of watching Charmaine being forced to stand on a chair with her hands tied behind her back with a leather belt, while Rose beat her with a wooden spoon. Charmaine's pitiful life came to an end in 1971. Fred was in prison at this time serving a short sentence for burglary and it is believed that Rose killed the 8-year-old during a savage beating. She hid the child's body until his release, when he removed her toes and fingers and buried her at 25 Midland Road, Gloucester, their home at that time. When her mother, Rena, came to visit her daughter, West murdered her and buried her in 'Letterbox Field', Much Marcle. Neither of them was ever reported missing and Charmaine's disappearance was easily explained. 'She's gone off with her mother,' said Rose.

Fred and Rosemary married in January 1972 and, following the birth of their second daughter, Mae, in June 1972, they moved into 25 Cromwell Street. This was their first real home and Fred and Rosemary were at last able to indulge their sadistic fantasies involving bondage and violence. The house became filled with whips and chains and other assorted paraphernalia. Fred fitted out the cellar as a torture chamber and 8-year-old Anne-Marie became a regular victim. She was violently raped by Fred while Rose held her down, threatening her with more violence if she told anyone. Rose was still operating as a part-time prostitute and had a red light outside her bedroom door, so that the children knew not to disturb Mummy when she was working.

In 1972 the Wests engaged 17-year-old Caroline Owens as a nanny. They drugged her, beat her and raped her. She promised not to tell anyone of her ordeal and incredibly they let her go. She reported the incident to the police and charges were brought against Fred and Rosemary. When the case came to court in 1973, Fred was able to convince the magistrates that Caroline had been a willing participant and both the Wests escaped with fines.

Number 25 Cromwell Street was a large house and they needed to take in lodgers to help meet the bills. In March 1973, 19-year-old Lynda Gough moved in. She was friendly with some of the Wests' other lodgers and had often been a visitor at the property. Within a few weeks she was dead. Her dismembered body was found underneath the bathroom floor, her head tightly bound with brown tape and her limbs piled on top of each other.

Over the next five years, Fred and Rosemary brutally murdered a further eight young women. They lured the girls back to Cromwell Street to use them in their sex games. Their victims would feel more secure in accepting lifts when Rose was in the car, never imagining that she not only indulged Fred's depravity but also embraced it herself, playing an active role in the torture and rape of their victims. Fred would often wrap the girls' heads in tape and force breathing tubes into their nostrils to prolong their agony while he indulged in all manner of sexual deviation in his torture chamber, even experimenting in bestiality and filming some of his exploits.

Victim Number Five was 15-year-old Carol Cooper. Living in a children's home at the time, Carol was last seen on 10 November 1973, catching a bus to visit her grandmother. Her remains were discovered on that fateful day in 1994, buried under the cellar floor at 25 Cromwell Street. West later admitted her murder, but denied Rose's involvement.

Driving home from a family Christmas visit on 27 December that same year, the Wests picked up 21-year-old Lucy Partington at a bus stop in Cheltenham. Lucy was from Gretton, Gloucestershire, and was studying medieval English at Exeter University. She vanished that night and her dismembered body was also found beneath the cellar floor in Cromwell Street. Fred checked into a local casualty department on 3 January 1974, with a deep cut to his hand, probably caused as he butchered his victim's corpse.

Therese Siegenthaler, a 21-year-old Swiss girl staying in London, was the next unfortunate victim. Her last known movements were hitch-hiking to Ireland for a holiday in 1974. Fred picked her up in his lorry near Chepstow and took her back to 25 Cromwell Street. Just like the other girls, she was incarcerated and subjected to a violent sexual attack before being murdered. Her body was found under the cellar. This time, some limbs were missing, possibly taken as gruesome souvenirs by Fred.

Shirley Hubbard was only 15 years old when she met her violent death in the Wests' torture chamber. She was on her way home to Droitwich by bus on 14 November 1974, but never arrived. Her body was uncovered with the others under the cellar floor, her head bound in tape and breathing tubes forced into her nostrils.

Fred decapitated his next victim, 18-year-old Juanita Mott, who was from Newent, Gloucestershire. Juanita was hitch-hiking through Gloucester on 11 April 1975, when the Wests offered her a lift. Reassured by the presence of Rose in the car, she made the worst decision of her life. The Wests bound her tightly with plastic clothes-line and, after using her in their usual depraved way, hammered her to death, removed her head and consigned her along with the others under the cellar floor.

Their next victim came to 25 Cromwell Street willingly. Shirley Robinson was one of their lodgers initially, helping out with babysitting. She fell in love with Fred and reputedly participated in three-in-a-bed sex sessions with Rose and Fred. When she fell pregnant with Fred's baby in 1978, Rose became jealous, despite the fact that she was also pregnant at the time with the child of a West Indian 'visitor'. Fred told his brother-in-law, Jimmy Tyler, that he was fed up with Shirley 'mooning' over him and that she would have to go. The body of Shirley and her unborn child was discovered buried in the garden at Cromwell Street.

Just a few months later, a replacement was easily found for Shirley. Sixteen-year-old Alison Chambers often visited a friend who lodged at Cromwell Street. Alison, originally from Swansea, Wales, lived in a children's home in Gloucester, and the Wests asked her to be their nanny and to move in. She was last seen on 5 August 1979. Her remains were also found in the garden.

Daughter Anne-Marie managed to leave the house of hell and moved in with a boyfriend. Fred switched his attentions to Heather and Mae and the sexual abuse continued. Heather suffered severe beatings but somehow managed to prevent Fred from raping her. However, she made the mistake of confiding in a friend. When she disappeared on 17 June 1987, questions were raised about her whereabouts. Friends and neighbours were told that she had run away, but this was one murder too many and people began to talk about the comings and goings at Cromwell Street. In fact, Heather was buried under the patio, a fate which was openly joked about between the Wests. Fred warned the other children that if they did not behave or co-operate, they would 'end up under the patio like Heather'.

The Wests were arrested in 1992 after allegations of child abuse had been brought against them. At the time, five of their children were under the age of 16 and were taken into care. Fred and Rose were charged with a series of sexual offences, including rape and buggery – but incredibly they escaped prosecution this time as the two main witnesses refused to testify.

One member of the investigating team could not let the case drop. Detective Constable Hazel Savage of Gloucestershire Police knew something was terribly wrong at 25 Cromwell Street. She managed to win the trust of the West children in care and gradually began to coax information out of them. They told her of Heather's disappearance, and the constant references to her being under the patio. Senior officers felt more evidence was needed before a search warrant could be granted, but Savage persisted and on 23 February 1994, the police finally began to uncover the grisly secrets within 25 Cromwell Street.

Following his arrest, West initially claimed he had committed all the murders himself and that Rose had had nothing to do with them. He also confessed to as many as twenty other bodies buried in various locations. He promised to give the police details of the locations, but, unfortunately for the families of missing girls, he committed suicide while in custody. He hanged himself on New Year's Day 1995 in his cell at Winson Green Prison, Birmingham, taking his secrets to the grave.

Rose initially denied any responsibility for the murders but her guilt was established when young Charmaine's remains were discovered, pinpointing the time of her death to 1971 – a period when Fred was serving a jail sentence. In October 1995, she was charged with ten murders. Anne-Marie gave evidence in court against her mother, describing the years of sexual abuse she had suffered from the age of 8. The strain of the trial proved too much for her on the second day that she was due to give evidence, and Anne-Marie took an overdose of pills. However, she summoned the courage to face her mother in court again, and on 23 November 1995, Rosemary West was found guilty of ten murders. She was sentenced to life imprisonment with Judge Mr Justice Mantell's recommendation that she never be released again.

The Wests won a firm placing in forensic psychiatrist Dr Michael Stone's 'Top Ten of Evil' – 'because they subjected their victims to the most prolonged torture in the most diabolical and physically and psychologically agonising way, with the total absence of remorse and the greatest glee'. He lists

Rosemary West as an 'almost equal' partner, adding that 'at least her husband had the decency to top himself'.

The police have always believed that many more young women met their deaths at the hands of the Wests. There was an eight-year gap between the murder of Alison Chambers in 1979 and that of Heather West in 1987 – but without the discovery of further bodies, the true extent of their crimes will never be known.

CHAPTER 3

Ted Bundy

'Hi, I'm Ted,' was chat-up line of the slick, sick charmer

He was as far from our idea of a homicidal maniac as it is possible to be. With drop-dead looks and whirlpool eyes, he was every girl's ideal date, every young male's ideal buddy, every mother's ideal son. The fact that such a handsome, dapper and charming man was secretly a savage, serial slayer makes the crime file on Theodore Robert Bundy all the more compelling.

There were few clues in young Ted's background to indicate the monster he would become. He was born on 24 November 1946, to 19-year-old Louise Cowell, of Philadelphia. The identity of the father forever remained a mystery but was believed to have been a member of the armed forces. Louise's parents, Sam and Eleanor, were both strict Methodists and, to avoid scandal, arranged for the birth to take place in a home for unwed mothers in Burlington, Vermont. Afterwards, mother and child returned to Philadelphia – but the grandparents pretended that the boy was their own adopted son.

Young Theodore grew up adoring his grandfather, a seemingly gentle landscape gardener who took the boy on trips to the coast, fishing in rivers or camping in the countryside. His relationship with his grandmother was less happy, however, since she suffered from depression and agoraphobia and ended up as a virtual recluse in their home.

While in the care of his grandparents, a disturbing incident occurred that may have revealed the boy's true character. His 15-year-old aunt later recalled how she had awoken one night to find that Ted had lifted the bedclothes and had been placing butcher's knives around her body. 'He just stood there and grinned,' she said. 'I shooed him out of the room and took the knives back to the kitchen. I remember thinking at the time that it was a very strange thing for a little kid to do.'

Ted took on the name Bundy after his mother, on the promise of a better job, uprooted with her son in 1950 and flew the 3,000 miles across America to Washington State where she met and married Johnnie Bundy, a cook at the Madigan Army Hospital, Seattle. The bridegroom adopted Ted and he grew up with them in their Tacoma home, where the couple had four more children of their own.

Young Ted became the all-American boy. He was active in a local church, serving as vice-president of the Methodist Youth Fellowship. He joined the Boy Scouts of America, did a paper round and undertook his own lawn-mowing business at weekends. A high school athlete, he won a place on the track team, before entering the University of Puget Sound, Seattle, and later switching to the University of Washington. He dropped out in 1967, preferring instead to enrol in a non-degree course in Chinese at Stanford University. He soon dropped out of that course, too, heading back to Seattle to spend the winter working odd jobs. He dabbled in politics, becoming a campaign worker for the Republican Party.

Bundy's butterfly mind, his inattentiveness and lack of direction may have been a clue to his character. So were his student reports, which spoke of a volatile temper. And although his undeniable charm and film-star looks won him no shortage of dates, some girlfriends recalled him as a sadistic lover who acted out weird bondage fantasies. Nevertheless, in 1971 he applied for voluntary work at a Seattle rape crisis centre and, after being screened for 'maturity and balance', he was accepted as a counsellor.

Crime writer Ann Rule, whose bestsellers have chronicled the worst in American criminal history, knew Bundy personally by working alongside him on the crisis hotline in the early 1970s. She later wrote: 'When people ask me about Ted, I wish I could show them this person that I knew who was everything you would expect a fine, 22-year-old guy would be. He was active in politics, wonderful on the phone, handsome, witty, charming. I was a friend of Ted Bundy's and I did not expect him to be a serial killer. When I last saw his face before he was executed, I saw this same kind of self-deprecating look, the duck of the head, the look that said, "You can believe this guy"'.

While working at the centre, Bundy wrote a pamphlet on rape that included this telling sentence: 'A number of rape offenders do not seem to be sick people but individuals who believe they can exert their will over others with impunity.' With hindsight, the thoughts he committed to paper were little more than an exercise in self-analysis. For although former colleagues at the time believed he could have ended up a leading lawyer, a top politician, perhaps even a Senator, Ted Bundy had almost certainly already embarked on his terrible career as one of the most feared serial killers in American history.

The total number of his victims will never be known, but at least thirty and as many as 100 unfortunate women and girls were murdered by Bundy. Officially, his killing spree lasted just four years – although Ann Rule is one of those who believed he may have started killing as far back as his teens. Bundy always denied this and, in Death Cell confessions, said he first tried to kidnap a woman in 1969 and committed his first murder in 1972.

However, Bundy's earliest known, identified murders were committed in 1974, when he was 27. In the early hours of 1 February 1974, he broke into the room of Lynda Ann Healy, a 21-year-old law student at the University of Washington, bludgeoned her unconscious, then dressed her in jeans and a shirt, and wrapped her in a bed sheet, before carrying her away. When college friends looked for her the following morning, they found a one-inch bloodstain on the pillow as the only sign that she had been there the previous night.

Girls now began disappearing at the rate of roughly one a month. On 12 March, Donna Gail Manson, aged 19, walked from her dormitory and headed across the Evergreen State College Campus, Olympia, to a student faculty music recital and was never seen again. On 17 April, Susan Rancourt, aged 18, left a meeting at the Central Washington University campus in Ellensburg to walk to a movie theatre 400 yards away. She too vanished.

Roberta Parks, aged 22, failed to return from a late-night walk on the campus of Oregon State University, in Corvallis, on 6 May. On 1 June, 22-year-old Brenda Ball walked out of a

Seattle bar with an unknown man and was never seen again. Georgeann Hawkins, aged 18, left her boyfriend's apartment on 11 June heading for her sorority house and was never seen again. A man with a plaster cast was seen in the area that night. He had asked another student to help him carry a briefcase to his car, a Volkswagen Beetle.

Bundy adopted the same subterfuge on 14 July – a day on which eight different people told of the handsome man with a VW Beetle who was seeking help because his arm was in a sling. The location was Lake Sammamish State Park, near Seattle, where, with temperatures in the nineties, a crowd of 40,000 were swimming and sunbathing. Among them was Janice Graham, a 22-year-old office worker, who came within seconds of dying at the hands of the killer and who was able to give a perfect description of Bundy. As she told police later, she was standing near the park's bandstand when a man in his mid-twenties approached her. She noticed that he was wearing jeans and a white T-shirt and his left arm was in a sling and plaster cast. He asked: 'Say, could you help me a minute? Would you help me put my sailboat on top of my car?' She agreed and he led her to a VW Beetle in the nearby parking lot. There was no sign of a sailboat, however, and Bundy explained: 'I forgot to say, it's at my folks' house just up the hill.'

It was the moment that Janice Graham hesitated, made an excuse and saved her life. 'I have to meet my husband,' she said, 'and I'm running late.' Afterwards, she recollected that the stranger was so charming that she had almost changed her mind again and gone with him: 'He was really friendly, very polite at all times, very sincere, easy to talk to. He had a nice smile.' Instead of falling prey to his charms, however, Janice walked back to the bandstand and watched fascinated as Bundy, having chatted up another girl, wandered with her towards his VW. 'A fast worker,' she thought.

Bundy's second target was also named Janice, a 23-year-old probation office worker named Janice Ott, who had been approached as she sunbathed. Witnesses who overheard their conversation recalled that a young man with his arm in a sling had introduced himself as 'Ted' and asked for help with his sailboat. Janice had smiled, stood up and wheeled her bicycle to where his car was. She was never seen alive again.

Later that day, Denise Naslund, an 18-year-old secretary, wandered with a party of friends to a nearby stream that ran into the lake. They swam together until late afternoon, when Denise left the water to walk to public restrooms. She became victim number eight. Two months later, on 7 September, a team of grouse-beaters found the remains of both Denise and Janice under a copse of trees. They had both been murdered in a sexual frenzy. Their bodies had also been stripped bare and their jewellery stolen. The body of a third woman found nearby could not be identified. The bodies of two more women were found by another hunter in the same area on 12 October. One of them was identified as Carol Valenzuela, aged 20, who had vanished on the Washington-Oregon border two months earlier. The other was never identified.

It was clear that, by mid-1974, Bundy had become sufficiently emboldened to operate by daylight and even to give his real name, introducing himself with the initial chat-up line: 'Hi, I'm Ted.' Detectives investigating the Lake Sammamish abductions discovered that several women had been approached there that same day by the handsome young man with his arm in a sling. The accurate descriptions of the killer and his car allowed the King County Major Crimes Unit to issue a public appeal, with drawings of their quarry. More than 3,000 callers telephoned the police hotline, one of them naming as a suspect a young law student named Ted Bundy. If he was ever checked out, he must have been placed close to the bottom of any list of suspects, as being above suspicion.

'Hi, I'm Ted' was now the greeting being used in fresh killing fields. On 30 August, Bundy quit his job at the Washington State Office of Emergency Services (putting on his resignation letter: 'The World Needs Me') and moved to Utah, where he enrolled at the University of Utah law school in Salt Lake City. Immediately, the killings began again, as the handsome charmer roamed new regions like some nomadic angel of death. The manner of these slayings was far from gentle. Typically, Bundy would bludgeon his victims, then strangle them to death. He also engaged in rape and necrophilia. His victims died in a sexual frenzy of such intensity that he was alternatively labelled the 'Werewolf Slayer', the 'Vampire Slayer' and the 'Ripper Slayer'.

On 2 September, while travelling from the West Coast to Utah, Bundy picked up a hitchhiker in Idaho, then raped and strangled her. He later confessed to the killing but her body was never found and her identity remains a mystery. Once in Utah, the killing continued. On 2 October 1974, Nancy Wilcox, aged 16, disappeared after accepting a lift in a VW Beetle. On 18 October, Melissa Smith, aged 18, was raped and murdered. On 31 October, 17-year-old Laura Aime was battered and strangled. Debbie Kent, aged 17, died on 8 November.

That same day, an attempt on the life of Carol Da Ronch, aged 18, failed after Bundy approached her in Murray, Utah, posing as a police officer. He told her that her car had been tampered with and asked her to accompany him to the police station. Once inside his Beetle, Bundy tried to slap handcuffs on her and, when that failed, tried to smash her skull with a metal bar. The quick-witted girl fought back and escaped by rolling out of the vehicle as it slowed at a bend.

From Utah, the slaughter spread to Colorado. Between January and July 1975, at least five women in that state went missing: Caryn Campbell, 23, on 12 January; Julie Cunningham, 26, on 15 March; Denise Oliverson, 25, on 6 April; Melanie Cooley, 18, on 16 April, and Shelly Robertson, 24, on 1 July. Yet police still had no clues as to the identity of the attacker, judging that, despite being a methodical killer, he must be a drifter who travelled from state to state, seeming to have no fixed abode.

The serial killer who had eluded capture for so long was finally trapped by that most mundane of police methods, the routine check. In the early hours of 16 August 1975, Highway Patrolman Robert Hayward was answering a routine call in his home town of Granger, Utah, when he saw a VW pull away from the kerbside in front of him at speed with no lights on. He forgot about the call-out and instead chased the car, his siren wailing. After twelve blocks, Ted Bundy stopped and Officer Hayward ran over to the VW, gun in hand. He questioned Bundy and asked him what he had inside his car. The killer replied: 'Just some junk.' The 'junk' turned out to be a pair of handcuffs, a crowbar, a ski mask and a nylon stocking.

Despite discovering what must have appeared to have been the tools of a burglar's or rapist's trade, Bundy was booked only for failing to stop for police and was immediately released on bail. It was not until the following day that he was arrested in his apartment at 565 First Avenue, Salt Lake City, and charged with possessing tools for burglary. The charge was a minor one but the net was closing. Carol Da Ronch, the girl who had escaped from Bundy's car when it slowed down, was re-interviewed and identified her assailant from the photograph on Bundy's driving licence. Recalled from bail, Bundy was put in an identification parade and was immediately picked out by Da Ronch.

Police could still not pin a murder rap on their prisoner, however. The charge now was kidnapping and of possessing tools for burglary. During months of legal argument, he was again set free on bail, which allowed him to return to his old hunting ground of Seattle before finally standing trial in Utah on 23 February 1976.

Jurors openly marvelled at the innocent-looking image of Ted Bundy when he finally faced his accusers. The smiling smooth-talker did his best to capitalise on that image, attempting to charm jurors into believing he had no need to kidnap and kill. As he boasted: 'Why should I want to attack women? I had all the female companionship I wanted. I must have slept with dozens and all of them went to bed with me willingly.'

Bundy, then aged 29, made a great impression in court. He was polite, well-spoken and utterly convincing. The case almost went his way. But he was found guilty of kidnapping and sentenced to between one and fifteen years. Relieved, police then moved their prisoner from Utah to Colorado to stand trial for the murder of 23-year-old student Caryn Campbell, abducted from a ski resort where Bundy had been prowling on the night of 12 January 1975.

It was there, incredibly, that Bundy again found freedom – not once but twice. During a break in the court hearing at Aspen, Bundy leaped from a window and was free for eight days before recapture. He escaped a second time by cutting through a ceiling panel of his cell and stealing a police car. He drove first to Chicago, then travelled south to Florida, and wherever he stopped, he took on a different identity. The killer was on top of the list of America's 'Most Wanted', yet he went unrecognised

when he rented a room near the University of Florida, Talla-
hassee, and again went on the rampage.

On 15 January 1978, he crept into a dormitory at the university and, wielding a heavy wooden club, viciously battered
four students, strangling two of them to death before taking
bites out the the buttocks of one of them. First to die was 21-
year-old Margaret Bowman. He beat her mercilessly and
strangled her with her own tights before taking bites out of her
buttocks. In the same way, he murdered Lisa Levy, aged 20. He
savagely beat two others, Karen Chandler and Kathy Keiner,
scarring both of them for life, before fleeing. Bundy's last victim
was his youngest. On 8 February, in Lake City, Florida, 12-
year-old Kimberly Leach was strangled and sexually violated.
Her body was left decomposing in a shed used for keeping pigs.

Luck finally ran out for the killer a week later. And again it
was not detectives' ingenuity but old-fashioned police patrol
work that caught him. In the early hours of 15 February, a
Pensacola policeman checked the number plate of a VW in a
restaurant car park and found that it had been stolen. The
driver identified himself as Ken Misner, which was one of
twenty-one identities that Bundy had assumed, complete with
matching credit cards, cheque books, passports and company
IDs. When questioned further, Bundy attacked Patrolman
David Lee and tried to escape but the officer clubbed him
unconscious. When Bundy came round, he told Lee: 'I wish
you would have killed me.'

Bundy was brought to trial in Miami accused of the Talla-
hassee student murders. Despite having the benefit of five
court-appointed lawyers, he insisted on acting as his own
attorney and cross-examined witnesses. He was convicted on all
counts. Confirming the death sentence, Judge Edward D.
Cowart made this extraordinary speech, proving that even the
judiciary could be impressed by the lethal charmer: 'It is
ordered that you be put to death by a current of electricity, that
current be passed through your body until you are dead. Take
care of yourself, young man. I say that to you sincerely; take
care of yourself, please. It is an utter tragedy for this court to see
such a total waste of humanity as I've experienced in this courtroom. You're a bright young man. You'd have made a good
lawyer, and I would have loved to have you practice in front of

me, but you went another way, partner. Take care of yourself. I don't feel any animosity toward you. I want you to know that. Once again, take care of yourself.'

Subsequently, in 1980, Bundy was convicted of the murder of 12-year-old Kimberly Leach. At that trial, jurors were shocked by evidence that bite marks on the child's body could only have been made by Bundy's teeth. He was found guilty and again sentenced to the electric chair.

Despite the horrific nature of his murders, Bundy began his long stay on Death Row in a cell stacked with messages of support and even proposals of marriage. He received sacks of mail from adoring women who could not believe that such a devastatingly handsome man could be responsible for such hideous crimes.

Bundy stalled his execution for almost ten years with a string of appeals which went as far as the US Supreme Court and cost the American taxpayer an estimated $7 million. But he finally confessed to thirty murders – for which, he said, 'I deserve to die' – including attacks in California, Michigan, Pennsylvania, Idaho and Vermont. Some were committed as 'day trips' with Bundy jetting into a city, selecting his victim, killing her and flying out again.

Time finally ran out for the notorious killer at Florida State Prison, at Starke, in January 1989. Religious broadcaster James Dobson spent the final night with him in his cell. Bundy refused his condemned man's last meal and wept openly as he told Dobson of his perverted sex drive. Dobson later wrote: 'Ted Bundy said society had a right to be protected from him. He said that after he killed the first woman he went through a period of great distress for six months. He was extremely guilty, he didn't believe he could have done something like that. But that gradually subsided and the sexual frenzy which he would go through occurred again and he killed another to sate it. Each time became a little easier to cope with and he did that so many times that he got to the point where he could not feel any more.'

At 7.06am on 24 January 1989, Ted Bundy was executed in the electric chair. The final thing he felt was the cold metal of the electrodes clamped to his leg. His last words were, 'I'd like you to give my love to my family and friends.' But outside the prison, his epitaph was more mocking. A crowd of several hundred revellers whooped 'Burn Bundy burn' and chanted: 'On top of Old Smokey, all loaded with juice, goodbye to old Bundy, no more on the loose!' A local DJ told listeners near the jail: 'Turn down your coffee makers folks because they're gonna need all the juice they can get there today.'

Finally, between 2,000 and 3,000 volts of electricity coursed through the killer's body for just under two minutes. He was pronounced dead at 7.16am. As his body was wheeled away on a trolley, Ted Bundy left a mystery for detectives and historians that may never be resolved. Did he commit the nine murders with which he was officially attributed or the thirty to which he had confessed or the 100-plus with which some investigators credit him? The generally agreed estimate is about thirty-five.

Theodore Bundy took with him to his ignominious end one other riddle . . . just what made Ted tick? What, within seconds, could turn this charming chancer into a vile and vicious killer? What changed the all-American boy with everything going for him into one of America's most reprehensible serial killers?

CHAPTER 4

Ivan Milat

Executions in the Australian Bush by the 'Backpack Killer'

Ivan Robert Marko Milat is regarded by many Australian criminologists as the most evil murderer the nation has ever spawned. He became known as the 'Backpack Killer' because of those he targeted: youthful adventurers travelling the world before settling down. As the bodies of his victims turned up in the years between 1989 and 1992, it became clear that a ritualistic serial killer was on the prowl, and Australian police received thousands of calls from worried parents around the globe who wanted assurance that their backpacking children were safe. Tragically, those who fell into Milat's clutches were never to return home ... having been executed in the most horrendously cruel manner.

Among those who learned the dreadful truth about the fate of their children were the parents of two British backpackers whose corpses were discovered deep in the Belanglo State Forest of New South Wales, at a site chillingly known as Executioners Drop, about 15 kilometres south-west of the town of Berrima.

Two men running along a forest track on 19 September 1992, had stopped to investigate a terrible stench. They were drawn to a large boulder where, below a pile of decaying leaves, they saw bone and hair. At first, they dismissed the find as a dead animal but changed their minds when they spotted a torn black T-shirt lying close by. Police were called and a widespread search was mounted, which the following day turned up a second body nearby.

The corpses were those of Britons Caroline Clarke, aged 21, and Joanne Walters, 22. Caroline had been stabbed and shot in the head several times. Joanne had been stabbed in the heart, lungs and her spine, probably paralysing her before the wounds that finally killed her.

Police first gave the terrible news to Joanne's parents, Ray and Jill Walters, already in the country searching for their missing daughter, and then telephoned Caroline's parents, Ian and Jacquie Clarke, in England. Before the girls' identities were publicly revealed, however, news that two bodies had been discovered caused the police to be inundated with phone calls from other parents whose student children had simply vanished on their Australian trekking holidays.

The fate of Caroline and Joanne had been particularly disturbing. The pair had disappeared five months before, last spotted alive in Sydney on 18 April after saying they planned to hitch-hike to Adelaide. It was not known where the killer had captured them but the attacks on the two girls had been frenzied and ferocious.

Caroline had also been stabbed and shot in the head several times. Bullet holes in a red cloth wrapped around her head showed she had been shot ten times. Disturbingly, when experts re-enacted the slaughter, they realised the bullets had been fired from several angles, suggesting the killer was using the girl as some sort of sickening 'target practice'.

Joanne had been stabbed in the heart and lungs, one cut going so deep it had penetrated her spine. Forensic pathologist Dr Peter Bradhurst was visibly moved when he had to report that the spinal wounds could have paralysed Joanne before the ones that finally killed her. She may also have been strangled. Joanne had been gagged and what was left of her hands still bore the jewellery she had been wearing.

Examination of the murder scene in Belanglo Forest revealed six cigarette butts, spent cartridges and a small piece of green plastic. Someone had also obviously built a fire from house bricks, an incongruous construction in a forest.

All these were clues to the killer. But what sort of man was he? Forensic psychiatrist Dr Rod Milton studied the crime scene to draw up a profile of him, and came to two firm conclusions: that the murderer was familiar with the area and that he had carefully planned what he intended to do. The killer's treatment of his victims showed he had wanted total control and there could be an underlying sexual motive. Dr Milton drew up a profile of the man he thought police should be hunting. He probably lived on the outskirts of a city in a semi-rural area and worked out of doors or in a semi-skilled job. He was unable to sustain a happy relationship and possibly had homosexual or bisexual tendencies. He would be in his mid-thirties and have a history of conflict with authority.

At this stage, however, there was no reason to believe the man they wanted was a serial killer. That confirmation came only a few weeks later. With few clues to the murders of Caroline and Joanne, police organised a public appeal for help at Bowral Town Hall at the end of September. One of those who attended, a man who had lived in the area all his life, was, as a consequence, extra vigilant as he drove through the Belanglo Forest some days later. His truck made its way along dirt tracks he knew well until he stopped at a burned-out fire in a clearing. Examining it with some foreboding, he noticed a bone sticking out of the ground. Parting some undergrowth, he then saw what was unmistakably a human skull.

Police were called and cordoned off the area and discovered not one but two corpses. They were the remains of James Gibson, and his girlfriend Deborah Everist, both 19 and from Victoria, who had disappeared while hitching a lift to a con-servation festival on 9 December 1989. All that police had been able to trace of them at the time was James's camera and back-pack which had been found on a roadside.

The young man's body was identified, though badly decom-posed. He had suffered the killer's 'trademark' knife wound through the spine; James's white canvas shoes were still laced up. A wider search revealed a black floppy hat – and the remains of Deborah Everist, a silver crucifix still around her neck.

Forensic pathologist Dr Peter Bradhurst was again in charge of determining how the two young people died. James had suf-fered deep spinal stabbings, similar to those of Joanne, which would have paralysed him before he was eventually killed. There were other stab wounds on the chest and ribs. The killer had slashed and slashed with some force. Deborah had suffered a single wound to the spine and slashes to the face and head.

The entire Belanglo State Forest now became a search area. By the end of October, they were ready to wind up the hunt, as there were just three square miles of the area left to search. But it was on this last patch that further grisly finds emerged. Another campfire was discovered, near to which were several items of women's clothing, including a pair of pink jeans. There was also a length of rope, an empty gun cartridge packet and tin cans shot through with bullet holes.

The next discoveries were a piece of leg bone with a brown boot attached and a human skull with a purple headband. The same fate as had befallen the others had been suffered by Simone Schmidl, a 21-year-old German girl missing for nine months. The trademark stabbing of the spinal column was obvious. In addition, Simone had been sexually assaulted. When discovered, her body was still partially dressed but her clothes had been pushed up in a position that suggested she had been molested.

Simone's distraught parents heard the news of the discovery on their radio before they were officially told by the police, who were awaiting formal identification. Simone had last been seen on 21 January 1991, hitch-hiking to Melbourne along the same stretch of road between Liverpool and Goulburn as James Gibson and Deborah Everist. Until then, the only trace police had of her were her glasses and camping equipment abandoned in the bush near the small town of Wangatta, Victoria.

Not all the clothing found at the scene was Simone's, however. The pink jeans matched that of another missing German backpacker, 20-year-old Anja Habschied. She and her 21-year-old boyfriend Gabor Neugebauer had been missing since December 1991. The last sighting of the couple was as they hitched lifts from King's Cross, Sydney, to Darwin.

What was left of Anja and Gabor was discovered a few days later, on 4 November 1992. Her head was missing, together with two of her vertebrae. Dr Peter Bradhurst, again on the case, was loath to release full details of Anja's death, for it appeared she had been decapitated while alive and in a kneeling position. Gabor had been gagged and strangled. His skull showed six bullet entries.

Police now knew they were dealing with a serial killer who, if not captured, would strike again and again. But although the method of the series of ritualistic murders was very similar, police believed that more than one person could have been responsible for them – a view still widely held. Equally, they felt that the killer (or killers) was getting confident, seemingly taking his time to slaughter his victims.

The manhunt now became a race against time. And the story became the most sensational that Australian crime reporters had tackled. Photographs of the victims were flashed on every TV screen and newspaper front page – and brought floods of calls from people who had seen them hitching their way around Australia. The story also brought a fresh flood of calls to police from worried parents around the world who wanted assurance that their backpacking children were safe. But news of the killing spree also brought the first substantial clue as to the identity of the perpetrator.

The person who provided police with the kind of information they so desperately needed was a British student, 20-year-old Paul Onions, who had been picked up by Ivan Milat and miraculously lived to tell the tale. On 25 January 1990, Paul had been hitching to find fruit-picking work in the Riverina district, several hundred miles south of Sydney. He had taken a train to Liverpool and was now thumbing lifts on the highway.

As he bought a cold drink from a roadside store, Paul was approached by a stranger offering him a lift. As he gratefully clambered into the man's four-wheel-drive vehicle, his supposed Good Samaritan introduced himself as 'Bill' and bombarded him with questions about where he was going and who might know of his whereabouts. But as they drove on, there was something about the man that made Paul feel uneasy. His fears were confirmed when Milat launched into a tirade about 'Pommies' and then said he needed to stop the vehicle to get some cassette tapes from the back. Paul noticed there was a large selection of tapes already neatly stacked in the front and decided that the man was acting so peculiarly that he should take to his heels.

With the vehicle at a halt, Paul started to get out – but was ordered back inside when the driver rounded on him with a pistol in his hand. Despite having a gun pointed at his head, Paul bravely made the decision to flee for his life. He fell into lines of traffic, desperately trying to get a car to stop. Even then,

Milat was determined not to let him go. He made one final dive for his intended victim but Paul managed to throw himself in front of a van, which stopped.

The driver, Joanne Berry, was just as terrified as Paul – for she thought she was being hailed by a madman. Her sister and four children were with her in the van, and she feared they were all in danger from Paul. But suddenly seeing a second man running towards her vehicle with a gun in his hand, Joanne let Paul stumble into the van and put her foot on the accelerator.

At Mittagong police station, Paul told his story, giving all the details he could remember. What he did not have was the vehicle's registration number. The duty police officer told him that without it there was very little chance of tracing his attacker – which, tragically for the other victims who followed, proved to be the case. Thus an opportunity to have forestalled Milat's killing spree was scandalously lost.

Equally wasteful were Paul's subsequent attempts to alert the police to the significance of his close encounter with the killer. When the hunt for the 'Backpack Killer' got under way almost three years later following the discovery of British girls Caroline Clarke and Joanne Walters, Paul Onions' experience should have provided instant, invaluable clues. Joanne Berry answered the police appeals to talk about her experience with Paul Onions. And Paul himself, now back in Britain but having seen the story in the newspapers, rang New South Wales Police on 13 November 1993, and begged for someone to take more seriously his report of the attack on him three years earlier. There was a third call, too, which should have made alarm bells ring. It was from a woman who said her boyfriend worked at the Readymix concrete company with a man who lived near a forest, drove a four-wheel-drive vehicle, owned a lot of guns . . . and was called Ivan Milat.

With more than 200 police officers searching the Belanglo Forest and with a flood of phone calls coming in, all of this important information was at first overlooked. The police computer system simply could not cope with the overload of information, and the manhunt began to falter in mid-November 1993. The 'Backpack Killer' task force streamlined the information process, whittling down the files until only those considered relevant were left. The huge stockpile of information now re-examined included Joanne Berry's report about how she had saved Paul Onions. But there were other vital statements that had also been overlooked.

One of these was from a 20-year-old woman who had told police she had been backpacking in New South Wales in January 1990 when she was offered a lift. The driver's behaviour gave her cause for concern and as they approached Belanglo Forest, the woman became very anxious. She managed to wrench open the vehicle's door and run into the forest – with the sound of gunshots close behind her. The woman was extremely fortunate to escape unharmed.

The investigation again went into top gear in December 1993 after a possible eighth victim was provisionally added to the 'Backpack Killer' list. An examination of unsolved murders turned up the name of Diane Pennacchio, a 29-year-old mother whose body had been found in a wood in 1991. She had been stabbed to death and her body had been laid face down with her hands tied behind her back. Her death was similar to the other seven forest murders because of the ferocious stab wounds and the fact Diane's body was found by a fallen tree and covered with twigs and ferns, another of the murderer's trademarks.

It was also about this time that police got round to investigating the previous tip from the woman who had told them her boyfriend worked at the Readymix concrete company with a man who lived near the forest, was a gun fanatic and who could easily be responsible for the forest murders – and she had actually named Milat. The woman had not given her name but two officers decided to pay the Readymix plant a visit. There they requested time sheets and found that Ivan Milat had been absent from work on the probable dates of the murders.

Why police should have overlooked the Milat tip-off for so long is astonishing – for he already had a criminal record. True, although he had served time in prison, there was nothing to suggest he was a potential serial killer. But there was on file an allegation that he had once raped a girl while armed with a knife and a length of rope.

Phone taps were made on Milat's home in Eagle Vale and a surveillance team kept him under constant observation. They discovered that Milat and two of his brothers owned another house just 25 miles from Belanglo Forest. Checks on vehicles Milat had owned showed that one of these was a four-wheel-drive Nissan Patrol in which the new owner had found a bullet.

The evidence clearly pointed to Milat. Yet the final link in the puzzle was not put into place until 13 April 1994, when an officer turned up Paul Onions' statement and realised its significance. Now back home in England but still deeply disturbed by what had happened to him, Paul was telephoned and asked to return to Australia. He immediately identified Ivan Milat from a photograph.

Police finally pounced in May 1994, with seven dawn raids on properties within a 50-mile radius of Belanglo Forest. Two of Milat's brothers were taken into custody but later released. Ivan Milat was arrested after police stormed his home at 22 Cinnabar Street, Eagle Vale, where he lay in bed with girl-friend Chalinder Hughes. He was taken to Campbelltown Police Station and charged with the robbery and attempted murder of Paul Onions.

Milat vehemently denied knowledge of the slayings but a search of his house produced items of property belonging to his victims, along with electrical tape, cable ties and a bag of rope similar to that found at the murder scenes. Gun parts were found hidden in the garage roof, together with cartridges that matched those found near the backpackers' bodies.

Charged with the seven murders, Milat first appeared in court in May 1994 but the hearing was postponed until the beginning of February 1995 when he was further remanded in custody until June that year. While the legal machinery ground slowly, the public learned a little more about the monster in their midst ...

Milat was born in 1945, one of fourteen children of a Croatian immigrant, Stijpan (who later changed his name to Stephen) and his wife Margaret. As a youth, he was an obses-sive body-builder but was less than superfit because of his heavy smoking and drinking. After leaving school, he took jobs on building sites to afford to pay for his passions for four-wheel-drive vehicles, hunting and shooting. He married but his wife Karen, a petite woman, suffered from Milat's violent outbursts.

He once smashed a glass coffee table and ordered her to pick up all the pieces. She left him in 1987 and psychologists suggested that, at this point in his life, Milat's aggressive nature became more terrifying and sinister.

Milat maintained his innocence throughout his trial, which finally began in March 1996 and lasted fifteen weeks. By now, seven murder charges had been added to the initial charge of the attempted murder of Paul Onions. The court was hushed as the jury heard of the injuries inflicted on the young victims and there were gasps when the sword used to decapitate Anja Habschied was produced.

His defence argued that, despite the horrific evidence presented to the jury, there was no actual proof that Ivan Milat was guilty. Suggestions were made that shifted the blame to other members of his family. The jury was not swayed. They found Milat guilty on all counts and he was sentenced to life imprisonment. He was taken to a high-security jail in Maitland, south-west of Sydney, bragging that he would one day escape. He made one failed escape attempt in July 1997.

As he began his sentence, speculation persisted that Ivan Milat had been aided in his crimes by one of his brothers. One of them, Boris, told reporters: 'All my brothers are capable of extreme violence, given the right time and place individually. The things I can tell you are much worse than what Ivan's meant to have done. Everywhere he's worked, people have disappeared. I know where he's been.' When asked if he thought Ivan was guilty, Boris replied: 'If Ivan's done these murders, I reckon he's done a hell of a lot more, maybe twenty-eight.'

In fact, the Australian press speculated that Ivan Milat's murder tally could be as high as thirty-seven. In June 2001, five years into his jail sentence, a closely-guarded Milat was brought from prison to appear at a reopened inquest into the deaths of three girls who had disappeared in 1978 and 1979 in similar circumstances to those surrounding his other victims. The killer refused to co-operate, and the deaths of the girls – 17-year-old Robyn Hickie, 14-year-old Amanda Robinson and 20-year-old Leanne Goodall – remained unattributed. However, he is still suspected of being responsible for many other murders, including those of tourists from Japan and throughout Europe.

Over the years, Milat continued to raise appeals against his conviction. Several times, he injured himself in prison, swallowing razor blades, staples and other metal objects. In January 2009, he cut off his little finger with a plastic knife, planning to mail it to the High Court. A support group continues to lobby for his release, and Milat himself still insists that he will one day escape – this time for good.

CHAPTER 5

John Wayne Gacy

Smell of death led police to morgue of the 'Killer Clown'

J ohn Wayne Gacy, the so-called 'Killer Clown', was anything but funny. Peculiar certainly, but there was nothing humorous about the mass murderer, whose past history gave a clear warning as to the monster he was to become. If, on the occasions of his earlier arrests, police had dug further into his background, they would have uncovered sinister clues to his evil character.

Gacy, born in Chicago in 1942, was the son of a Danish mother and Polish father who was abusive towards him. John Gacy Sr was an alcoholic who gave his son constant beatings, sometimes even hurling him across the room in drunken rages. Labelled a 'dumb sissy' by his father, young John was a sickly child. He suffered from dizzy spells in his youth, supposedly the result of being hit on the head by a swing at the age of 11. Blackouts continued throughout his teens until a blood clot on the brain was diagnosed and successfully treated. While suffering his father's wrath, John allowed himself meekly to be dominated by his mother and older sister and psychiatrists believe this may have led to a resentment of women that influenced his later behaviour.

Despite the early traumas, Gacy nevertheless completed a good education at business school, moving to Iowa and becoming a top salesman with the Nunn-Bush Shoe Company. While in that job, in 1964 he met and married fellow employee Marlynn Myers, who described him as 'a likeable salesman who could charm anything right out of you'. His bride's parents owned a fried chicken restaurant, which Gacy successfully managed. The couple had two children and settled down to family life, Gacy apparently a pillar of the local community in the city of Waterloo, being a leading light in the Junior Chamber of Commerce.

Disturbing forces were coming to the surface, however. In 1968, he sexually assaulted a young male employee at the restaurant. The terrified boy was handcuffed while 20-stone Gacy subjected him to a vicious attack. The boy fought back against attempts to sodomise him and force him to perform oral sex and afterwards went to the police. The town was shocked when Gacy was charged with homosexual acts, although a further charge of hiring a thug to beat up the prosecution witness was dropped when Gacy plea-bargained himself a charge of sexual molestation and he was given a sentence of ten years' imprisonment.

Gacy served only eighteen months, his reputation as a model prisoner convincing his parole board that he was no longer a risk to the public, but it was long enough to send his life into a tailspin. His wife divorced him, taking their two children, so he moved back to his home-town of Chicago. He settled in the suburb of Des Plaines, where he launched a successful construction business and worked hard to regain his social standing. He became involved in the local political scene, campaigning for the Democratic Party and was once photographed with President Jimmy Carter's wife Rosalynn. And in his spare time he performed as 'Pogo the Clown' at charity events and children's parties.

Photographs of him in that role would later earn him the nickname 'Killer Clown'. But, for the moment, it helped disguise Gacy's true nature. In 1971, only a year out of jail and while still on parole, he was questioned by police for trying to force a teenaged boy into having sex. The case had to be dropped after the boy failed to turn up for the preliminary hearings. Gacy's parole officers in Iowa were not informed of the arrest, so the sexual deviant was formally discharged from parole later that year.

In 1972, Gacy was married a second time, to Carole Hoff, but this also ended in failure and she walked out on him in 1976. Police were later to learn how Hoff was puzzled by his lacklustre sexual performance and terrified of his violent temper. Like his first wife, Carole said that Gacy had acted normally during the first few months of the marriage but had then begun to behave mysteriously, staying out all night in his car. Just before they separated, he had 'started bringing home lots of pictures of naked men'. Carole also said that she had complained constantly to her husband about the fetid smell that seemed to hang around the house.

The reason for the odour would not become clear for another two years, during which pornography-addicted Gacy remained on the loose as a predatory serial killer. Shamefully for the police, one incident that could have stopped him in his tracks went largely unpunished. In March 1978, a 27-year-old Chicago man, Jeffrey Rignall, went to the police with an horrific story. He told them how he had been approached by a fat man driving a distinctively-coloured Oldsmobile car. Invited to sit in the passenger seat for a smoke of cannabis, he had been rendered unconscious when a chloroformed handkerchief was held to his face.

Rignall remembered regaining consciousness in the basement of his abductor's house where he was bound fast to a home-made torture device which the fat man, who now stood before him naked, referred to as 'the rack'. Weird sexual implements were used on the terrified hostage and the pain was so severe that he prayed that he would die quickly, but the torture continued for hours, with repeated whippings and rapes. Rignall told detectives that the fat man had boasted that he was a policeman and that he 'would just as soon shoot you as look at you'.

The dazed kidnap victim earned his freedom by promising that he would leave Chicago if Gacy would release him. Strangely, he did, and the following morning he was dropped off in Chicago's Lincoln Park. He was more dead than alive but was fully clothed, with his money and wallet still on him. Taken to hospital, he was found to be suffering from severe mental trauma. He was bruised and bleeding internally, and he had suffered permanent liver damage as a result of the chloroform he had inhaled.

Despite his injuries and the detailed description of the horrific crimes, Rignall failed to convince police to instigate a full investigation. Instead, an incensed Rignall turned detective himself and launched his own search for Gacy's car. Crisscrossing the city's streets, his persistence paid off when the vehicle passed him as he staked out an expressway exit that was the only landmark he recalled from his journey in a chloroform-induced coma. He took down the licence plate details and followed the Oldsmobile until it turned into the driveway of an expensive ranch-style home at 8213 West Summerdale Avenue, Des Plaines. Fearful to approach the occupant, he checked through real estate records until he established that the owner was 36-year-old John Wayne Gacy Jr.

Surely now police would act, Rignall thought. Yet when he went back to them with all this information, the frustrated victim was told it was not enough. He begged detectives to question Gacy – but it took them four months to get round to doing so. They visited Gacy's home in July 1978 but, since there were no other witnesses than Rignall to challenge his statements and alibi, the incident resulted in only a mis-demeanour charge. That case dragged on for a further five months – and was never concluded because, by then, Gacy had struck again and been exposed as a mass murderer.

The tragic victim was 15-year-old Robert Piest, who left his family home in Des Plaines on the evening of 11 December 1978, to attend a job interview in order to earn some extra cash for the school vacation. His appointment was for 9.00pm at the local pharmacy where his prospective employer, a building contractor, was carrying out renovation work.

As he stepped out of the front door, his mother urged him to return speedily. It was her birthday and a family party was getting into full swing. When there was still no sign of Robert by midnight, his worried mother phoned the police to report that he had not returned. He never did.

As soon as police established the identity of the builder Robert had been due to meet, they realised that this was not simply a 'missing persons' case. John Wayne Gacy had a long criminal record as a sexual deviant. Detectives who questioned him found his answers unconvincing and, although there was no evidence to arrest him, they asked the local force to place him under close surveillance. Despite knowing that he was being watched, Gacy managed to remove Piest's body from West Summerdale Avenue and dump it in the Des Plaines River. In fact, it was this boldness that was finally his undoing. On 19 December, Gacy boldly invited the officers sitting outside his home to pop in for a cup of coffee. The cops immediately smelled a strong odour, which Gacy put down to a drainage problem. But the smell that hung around had an awful familiarity. A warrant was obtained and Gacy was arrested as police began a search of the house.

When they lifted the trapdoor that led to the crawl-space beneath the floorboards, officers discovered one of the most gruesome scenes in the history of American crime. Stored in the cramped void were seven corpses in varying stages of decomposition. More were dug out of crude lime pits in the garden. In total, the remains of twenty-nine bodies, mainly teenaged boys, were found in the house and grounds. The victims ranged in age between 9 and their mid-20s. Some were homosexuals and some were men who had worked for, or sought work from Gacy. All had endured savage sexual torture. Gacy confessed that he had run out of space to store any more corpses. Another five victims, including Robert Piest, had been thrown into the Des Plaines River. Nine of the victims were never identified.

Although Gacy bore all the signs of a homosexual in denial, he adamantly denied any gay leanings. In fact, his sole explanation for his crimes was a hatred of homosexuals. Once he had raped his victims, he felt easy about killing them 'for their homosexual activities' – this despite the fact that several of his victims were heterosexual. A number of them had, like poor Robert Piest, been 'straight' males who had come to Gacy simply wanting a job.

Over months of questioning, Gacy admitted his crimes and described how he would frequent Chicago's Greyhound Bus Station looking for drifters to whom he would offer jobs with his construction company. 'I wanted to give these people a chance,' he said, 'because young folk always get a raw deal. If you give them responsibility, they will rise to the occasion. They are hard workers and proud of their work.' Some were indeed offered jobs. Others died even before seeing the construction site.

Another of Gacy's hunting grounds was Chicago's notorious 'Bughouse Square' where itinerants and rent boys hung out. He would invite a victim to accompany him back home, where he displayed a collection of police equipment, including badges and handcuffs. Gacy would offer to show his unsuspecting visitor the 'handcuff trick' which, he said, would have him released within seconds. Once trapped, however, Gacy would bind the terrified captive to his torture rack and violently sodomise him. Afterwards, Gacy would often garrotte his captive by tying two knots in a length of cord, circling it round the victim's neck, then twisting it tight with a piece of wood. Death might take several minutes.

Gacy pleaded not guilty by reason of insanity at his trial in Chicago in February 1980. District Attorney William Kinkle described Gacy as a sick man who methodically planned and executed his many murders. The State of Illinois was at that time debating the reintroduction of the death penalty, and Kinkle asked that this be Gacy's fate. The defence lawyers' plea of insanity was rejected and, on 12 March 1980, the jury convicted him of murder and he was sentenced to death. He survived for fourteen years on Death Row through a long string of appeals. John Wayne Gacy Jr was finally executed by lethal injection at Stateville prison, near Chicago, on 10 May 1994. His last reported words to a warder were: 'Kiss my ass.'

CHAPTER 6

Marc Dutroux

Young girls starved to death in killer's secret dungeon

Murdering monster Marc Dutroux may have been under police surveillance but somehow he slipped through the net and was allowed to kidnap and kill. The crimes became one of the greatest blights on Belgian legal history, with disturbing accusations of incompetence and even of a cover-up within the legal system. By the time Dutroux came to court in 2004, the whole world had learned of his horrific deeds. And it was a waiting world, too, that witnessed the beast sentenced to life. After a sixteen-week trial, a Belgian jury convicted the unemployed electrician of kidnapping, raping and killing girls over a period of eight years.

In 1995, police raided Dutroux's house after a tip-off that he had dug a dungeon in which to imprison girls. Once indoors, the officers thought they could hear screaming – believed to be that of incarcerated and terrified 8-year-olds Julie Lejeune and Mélissa Russo. But the police accepted Dutroux's explanation that the cries came from children playing in the street – and, scandalously, both girls were left to die. This was one of the bleak oversights that would later see the state prosecutor, whose investigation finally freed the last two girls Dutroux abducted, hounded by death threats and eventually taken off the case.

Little Julie and Melissa were Dutroux's first victims, snatched from near their homes in Eastern Belgium in June 1995. The monster had been out of prison for three years, having served only three years of a thirteen-year sentence for a string of rapes. He should, by rights, have come under police suspicion almost immediately. But two months after abducting the two girls, Dutroux kidnapped 17-year-old An Marchal and 19-year-old Eefje Lambrecks from the Belgian coastal town of Ostend where the teenagers were on holiday. Their bodies were later found beneath a shed on Dutroux's property – and subsequent forensic evidence suggested that they had been buried alive. Incredibly, even though Dutroux had been imprisoned previously for raping young women and was under police surveillance at the time of these abductions, he was never taken in for questioning.

Fate was particularly cruel to Julie Lejeune and Mélissa Russo. For Dutroux was sent to prison for three months following the theft of a car in December 1995. He left instructions with his then wife, Michelle Martin, to keep the little girls locked in his dungeon and feed them. She failed to do so and the girls starved to death. In court, Martin testified that she had been afraid to look in the dungeon. But she did feed Dutroux's two dogs ...

When Dutroux got out of jail, he buried the girls in the backyard of another of his properties, where an accomplice, Bernard Weinstein, was living. Later, he also killed Weinstein and buried him in the yard too. The reason, he told police, was that Weinstein had failed to feed the girls while he was in jail. The way he disposed of his former friend was typically horrific. Dutroux crushed Weinstein's testicles until he revealed the hiding place of some money, then drugged him and buried him alive.

Despite a police report that Dutroux was interested in abducting juvenile females, and despite a national campaign led by An Marchal's father to find the four missing girls, Dutroux felt confident enough to strike again. He kidnapped Sabine Dardenne, then aged 12, on 28 May 1996, as she was cycling to school in the Belgian city of Charleroi. The girl was grabbed by Dutroux and stuffed inside a trunk in his van before being taken back to his prison-house, chained to a bed by her neck and ordered to undress. She was raped as many as twenty times and photographed.

Dutroux also began a sickening assault on the child's mind as well as her body. He told her he was working as part of a team and that his 'boss' wanted her dead because her parents were not prepared to pay the 3 million-franc ransom that would spare her life. Dutroux asked Sabine if she wanted to live or die. If she chose to live, she would have to remain in the cramped 3ft × 9ft dungeon because if the 'boss' found out where she was, he would kill her and her parents. Sabine asked to live and was imprisoned in the dungeon with only a filthy mattress and a handful of crayons, which Dutroux cruelly told her to use to write letters to her parents. They were never posted, of course, and Dutroux callously fabricated replies from Sabine's mother. He told the girl: 'She says to make sure you eat properly, that you were never much good at washing yourself and that you should enjoy the sex.'

On 9 August 1996, Dutroux kidnapped 14-year-old Laetitia Delhez as she made her way home from the local swimming pool and drove her to the house where Sabine was being kept. But a witness to her abduction noted the number plate of Dutroux's van, leading to his arrest on 13 August. Police at first found no sign of the girls at the house. It was two days later, when Dutroux confessed to the crimes, that he led them to Sabine Dardenne and Laetitia Delhez, who were miraculously found alive in the basement.

Dutroux's trial began in Arlon, the capital of the Belgian province of Luxembourg, on 1 March 2004, some seven and a half years after his initial arrest. While admitting abduction charges, Dutroux denied the three murder charges against him – of killing An Marchal, Eefje Lambrecks and Bernard Weinstein, whose murder he had originally admitted. He was also charged with a host of other crimes including theft, abduction, attempted murder and attempted abduction, molestation, and three unrelated rapes of women from Slovakia.

It was a trial by jury and up to 450 people were called upon to testify. One witness alleged that satanic ceremonies were used to 'welcome' new victims with the aim of disorienting them, making them doubt the reality of their memories and prevent them from disclosing the abuse.

The trial was not only a horrific tale of one man's violence and violation against girls but one of suggested intervention from higher levels. As the trial was starting, a key that fitted Dutroux's handcuffs was found hidden in a container of salt in a cupboard near his prison cell. He briefly made his escape before being recaptured. This led to Dutroux feeding conspiracy theories that he was part of a paedophile ring that supplied girls for wealthy clients. But evidence of a wider ring was never found. High-level resignations were handed in, including the Minister of Justice, Stefaan De Clerck, the Minister of the Interior, Johan Vande Lanotte, and the police chief.

One of those called to the witness stand was Jean-Marc Connerotte, the original judge of the case, who was dismissed after it was revealed he had been hosted for dinner by one of the victim's parents. Connerotte broke down in tears when he described the bullet-proof vehicles and armed guards needed to protect him 'against shadowy figures' determined to stop the full truth coming out. He said: 'Never before in Belgium has an investigating judge at the service of the king been subjected to such pressure. We were told by police that murder contracts had been taken out against the magistrates.' Connerotte testified that the investigation was seriously hampered by protection of suspects by people in the government. 'Rarely has so much energy been spent opposing an inquiry,' he said, adding that he believed the Mafia had taken control of the case.

During his trial, the court heard about 47-year-old Dutroux's past and how his parents had separated when he was still young. Dutroux had stayed with his mother and had worked briefly as a male prostitute before marrying at the age of 19. He had fathered two children before the marriage ended in 1983. Dutroux's life of crime began in 1979 when he received his first convictions for minor offences. His twenty-five-year run of crimes went on to include violent mugging, drug-dealing and car theft. It was the spoils of all this that enabled Dutroux to purchase seven properties – one containing the prison he had built with his bare hands and hidden behind a wall in the basement.

Dutroux met Michelle Martin and married her while both were serving time in prison. The couple went on to have three children. In 1986 they were jailed for the kidnapping and rape of five young girls. Dutroux was released after three years when it was deemed he was no longer a threat to children. This was despite a warning from his own mother, who said she was concerned her son was keeping young girls at his house. She also wrote to the prison director saying: 'What I do not know, and what all the people who know him fear, is what he has in mind for the future.' The letter was apparently ignored. Following his release, Dutroux was able to convince a psychiatrist that he was disabled, allowing him to claim a government pension. He also received sleeping pills and sedatives, which he would later use on the abducted girls.

In June 2004, Dutroux was found guilty of the murders of An Marchal, Eefje Lambrecks, and Bernard Weinstein, all of whom, it was suggested, had been drugged and buried alive. Dutroux was also found guilty of kidnapping and raping the two girls who survived. Their testimony and their return with the jury to the dungeon where they had been held provided the most dramatic moments of the trial. Dutroux was sentenced to life in prison. His 44-year-old former wife – having wed while both were in prison, they divorced in 2003 while both were in prison – was sentenced to thirty years in prison for causing the death of Julie Lejeune and Mélissa Russo.

There were two others in the dock. An accomplice of Dutroux who was described as his 'faithful companion', Michel Lelièvre, 33, was sentenced to twenty-five years for complicity in the kidnappings and other charges. And a businessman, 63-year-old Michel Nihoul, was sentenced to five years for helping smuggle drugs and people into Belgium. It was Nihoul whom Dutroux had implicated in the link between himself and an international ring of paedophiles, which included police officers, businessmen, doctors, and even high-level Belgian politicians. Nihoul was acquitted of kidnapping and rape after the jury failed to reach a verdict on those charges.

The judge, Stéphane Goux, who was criticised for his handling of the trial, said in the nationally broadcast proceedings that he hoped the sentence would offer Dutroux's two surviving victims a chance to 'move on'. After the sentences were passed, Louisa Lejeune, mother of little Julie said: 'A page has turned. It is recognition of what happened and that comes as a relief.' Added An's father, Paul Marchal: 'I am happy. They are guilty for everything that they have done.'

Martin and Lelièvre could eventually win reduced sentences for good behaviour, a fact that disturbed Jean-Denis Lejeune, Julie's father. He said: 'These people kidnapped children, tortured them and left them to starve.' Under Belgian law Dutroux's sentence can be reviewed in twenty years, but few believe that the most reviled paedophile in Europe will ever be freed.

A 17-month investigation by a parliamentary commission into the Dutroux affair produced a report which concluded that, while Dutroux did not have accomplices in high positions within the police and justice system, as he continued to claim, he profited from corruption, sloppiness and incompetence. But there was still speculation as to the motivation behind Dutroux's abduction and imprisonment of young girls.

It was strongly rumoured that Dutroux had offered money to a police informer for providing girls and had even told him that he was constructing a cell in his basement. The killer's mother had also written a second letter, this time to the police, claiming that Dutroux held girls captive in his houses. One newspaper reported: 'While Dutroux's trial is over, it will take years to wash away the stain the case has left on Belgium's police and judicial systems, which fumbled it so badly that many people said they believed there was a high-level effort to protect him from prosecution.'

CHAPTER 7

Michel Fourniret & Monique Olivier

Sick lust of the vile couple who went hunting for virgins

It was a chilling and sinister sobriquet: 'The Ogre of the Ardennes'. But if Michel Fourniret, 65, deserved it for murdering a series of young women, then his wife, Monique Olivier, 59, should be dubbed 'The Ogress of the Ardennes' for her part in not only securing the hapless victims, but for witnessing their vile deaths too.

The Fournirets' terrifying reign of slaughter came to light in May 2004 – coincidentally as Belgian magistrates were concluding another high-profile case: that of notorious paedophile Marc Dutroux (*see* Chapter 6). Also a known paedophile, French forest warden Fourniret confessed to murdering and sexually assaulting seven virgins in France and Belgium over a sixteen-year period. Some four years later, Fourniret completed his notoriety by being convicted not only of the murder, rape and attempted rape of those seven, but also being strongly suspected of the murder of other victims – something which was to make him one of France's worst-ever serial killers.

The victims, mostly French girls aged between 12 and 21 were either strangled, shot or stabbed with a screwdriver. They were carefully selected in a series of murders between 1987 and 2000 to satisfy Fourniret's sick lust for sexually inexperienced females.

Fourniret had certainly not confessed to his crimes for any compassionate reason. His murder spree only stopped in 2003 when a 13-year-old girl he had kidnapped in Belgium managed to escape from his van and made a note of the registration number. Detectives arrested the couple but did not at first realise they were dealing with serial killers. That only became clear when Olivier gave information to the police after hearing of the thirty-year sentence given to Dutroux's wife Michelle Martin for her part in their crimes. Olivier believed that co-operating with the police would spare her, particularly as she denied any involvement with her husband's murders. A court was later to hear differently ...

By the time he was arrested, former school supervisor Fourniret had already served three years of a seven-year sentence for trying to abduct a 13-year-old Congolese girl in 2003. She said she had been bundled into his van after he asked for directions. Unbeknown to the authorities, however, this had not been the first time Fourniret had pounced.

During his time in prison, Fourniret became friendly with a cellmate, bank robber Jean-Pierre Hellegouarch, who unwisely revealed to him the whereabouts of his stash – a secret he had already confided to his wife Farida. Once freed, Fourniret went to the appointed spot with Farida and dug up the money. He then killed Farida and moved with his wife to the village of Sart-Custinne on the Franco-Belgian border, where he purchased a château. The château's grounds were to be the burial site of at least two of Fourniret's victims, their bodies discovered on 3 July 2004 by a team of French and Belgian police.

It is believed that Fourniret's serial killings had begun in December 1987 when he kidnapped, raped and murdered 17-year-old Isabelle Laville as she walked home from school in the French Burgundian town of Auxerre. Years later, in July 2006, Fourniret led investigators to her skeletal remains, buried at the bottom of a well in north-eastern France. His next murder was that of 20-year-old Fabienne Leroy, who was snatched from a supermarket car park outside Paris in July 1988. Her body was later found outside a nearby military base with a shotgun wound to the chest.

Fourniret's youngest victim was a 12-year-old Belgian girl, Elisabeth Brichet, who disappeared after playing with a friend in Namur in 1989. It was later revealed that Olivier helped to trap the child so that Fourniret could strangle her. Elisabeth's disappearance was long thought to be at the hands of Marc Dutroux – until Fourniret led police to her burial site on his estate.

Olivier was also the accomplice in Natacha Danais's killing. The 13-year-old teenager was kidnapped, sexually assaulted and stabbed to death near Nantes, western France, in November 1990. Her body was found three days later on a beach on the French Atlantic coast. Fourniret and Olivier had lured Natacha into their van, again from a supermarket car park, and Fourniret had stabbed her during an attempted rape. Later, the coroner suggested a sexual assault had taken place after the girl's death.

Other victims were Jeanne-Marie Desramault, a 22-year-old French student who disappeared from the railway station of Charleville-Mézières in 1989. Her body was recovered from the estate of Fourniret with his assistance; 18-year-old Céline Saison who disappeared in Sedan in 2000 and whose body was found in Belgium; 13-year-old Manyana Thumpong who disappeared from Charleville-Mézières in 2001 and whose body was also found in Belgium.

Fourniret's wife has claimed that in 1993 he also killed a Belgian 16-year-old who had worked as an *au pair* at their house. She said she had come home to find her husband and the girl naked and that he had strangled her. Fourniret himself confessed to killing a man in a robbery in a French lay-by in the 1980s, simply because he needed some quick cash.

During the couple's trial, which started on 27 March 2008, at Charleville-Mézières, north-east France, state prosecutor Francis Nachbar described Fourniret and Olivier as 'inhuman and cruel criminals, the likes of which our country could have never imagined'. He called the serial killer a 'necrophiliac monster' and said that, together with Olivier, they formed a 'devil with two faces'.

The court heard the evidence of one girl who had been fortunate enough to escape from the couple's clutches. She said Fourniret had boasted that he was 'far better' than fellow paedophile and serial killer Marc Dutroux. Throughout, Fourniret showed no remorse for his crimes. During his trial, he said that he would not apologise for them, and went on to make a series of bizarre requests – demanding, for instance, that women on the jury certify that they were virgins at marriage. However, detectives said that behind the arrogant façade, Fourniret was concerned that the trial might delve into things he would prefer to hide, notably his problem with premature ejaculation. Some of his victims were not sexually molested but Fourniret ejaculated over them.

The jury was shocked to hear evidence that Olivier, accompanied by her baby son Selim, was regularly used as a lure to put potential victims at ease. Once a young girl was earmarked for abduction, the couple would pose as lost motorists asking for directions. Fourniret would then kidnap his victims and order Olivier to watch him rape and kill them. Olivier later admitted in court that she and Fourniret would re-enact scenes from their crimes while having sexual intercourse.

This was all a horrific change of character for the ex-nurse and mother of a baby who had no criminal record prior to meeting Fourniret. Olivier had met him in 1986 after replying to his advert for a pen pal while he was in prison serving a sentence for sexual assault. After forming a relationship, the two made a pact that Fourniret would kill Olivier's former husband if she assisted in finding virgins to violate and murder. And although Fourniret reneged on his promise, such was his hold over Olivier that she kept her part of the bargain.

Fourniret himself admitted in court that he had a sexual obsession with virgins and, although not showing remorse, stated: 'I remain an extremely dangerous individual.' The trial ended on 28 May 2008, with Fourniret being sentenced to life imprisonment. This was despite a vain plea by his lawyer Pierre Blocquaux to show compassion towards his client. 'Whatever he has done,' said the lawyer, 'this is a man we are judging. He is part of our humanity, alas, regardless of the horrible nature of these acts.' Monsieur Blocquaux added that the trial also laid bare some of the 'tragic' police errors that enabled Fourniret to avoid arrest for years – both in France and across the border in Belgium. In particular, there had been no communication between the police and the gendarmerie, run by different ministries.

In the case against Fourniret's wife, lawyers representing her argued that the slight woman was the weak and fearful wife of an overpowering and violent husband, who would have killed her and their son if she had refused to take part in his sex and blood lust. But state prosecutor Xavier Lenoir described Olivier as a willing accomplice, a 'bloody muse' and a 'deceitful witch' who displayed 'a deafening silence' to the screams of girls being raped by her husband. Olivier was sentenced to thirty years' imprisonment, with no possibility of parole before serving a minimum of twenty-eight years. The only pity for her victims was expressed in the words: 'I regret everything that I have done. That is all.'

The parents of the victims were given the chance to vent their rage during the trial, to which they turned up carrying white roses in memory of the seven. 'I feel so much hate that if life permits, I will go and spit on your grave,' said the father of Céline Saison.

Although Fourniret was convicted of the murder, rape and attempted rape of seven people, he was actually accused of killing ten – nine in France and one in Belgium. It is believed the tally of his victims is higher and includes the 1990 killing of British student Joanna Parrish, 20, who was working as a teaching assistant in Burgundy when she was raped and murdered near Auxerre. The Leeds university student had answered a newspaper advert placed by a man seeking someone to give his son English lessons. Joanna's naked body was later found floating in a river. She had been strangled. Her parents, Roger Parrish and Pauline Sewell, who sat in on part of the Fournirets' trial, campaigned for eighteen years against what they saw as police blunders, delays and inexplicable legal barriers in tracking down their daughter's killer. After her arrest, Olivier had recounted a murder to police which had remarkable similarities to that of Joanna.

Fourniret denied committing any crimes between 1990 and 2000 but the police in France, Belgium, Holland, Germany and Denmark looked back at rape cases, disappearances and murders which lay on their files. Despite similarities in the method or murder, police were unable to definitely link Fourniret to a rape in Denmark and the disappearance of two girls, Tanja Groen and Nicky Verstappen, in Holland.

In 2006, speculation was rife that Fourniret was the real perpetrator of the Marseille murder of 8-year-old Marie-Dolores Rambla in June 1974. Another man, Christian Ranucci, had been convicted of the crime and beheaded in July 1976. The conviction and death sentence has always been shrouded in controversy, but new evidence showed that Fourniret was on holiday in Marseille at the same time and place when the girl was murdered. Marie-Dolores and her brother Jean were stopped by a man in a car who claimed he was searching for his dog. Marie-Dolores was abducted and her fatally-stabbed body was later found in bushes. Ranucci was arrested as he was seen carrying a large package and admitted killing the girl – only to withdraw the confession later.

There were subsequent media suggestions that Ranucci's file was altered and certain pieces of evidence were hidden to match his 'confession'. Blood found in Ranucci's car was said to be that of Marie-Dolores but further investigation revealed both shared the same blood type. An elderly couple who claimed they saw Marie-Dolores in the back of Ranucci's car and heard her screaming had not actually left their own car to get a good look. Five further witnesses to the kidnapping could not identify Ranucci. Ranucci's car door was broken on the side they claimed he had opened to snatch the girl. And further investigation showed that a red sweater found at the scene of the crime did not belong to Ranucci, as previously thought.

Three decades after the executioner probably put paid to the wrong man, the likelihood that evil Fourniret was the real killer of Marie-Dolores grew more compelling. Fourniret had been in the area, had been driving a grey car as described by the witnesses ... and the 'lost dog' story was one of the ploys he used to ensnare his young victims.

CHAPTER 8

Lawrence Bittaker & Roy Norris

Kidnappers who garrotted teen victims with wire and pliers

I f ever the clearest warning signs were ignored, it was in the case of Lawrence Bittaker. Psychiatrists correctly categorised him as a habitual, violent, paranoid criminal with a hatred of women. They labelled him a 'sophisticated psychopath' who should never be freed. Yet freed he was, and five victims paid the ultimate price for officialdom's leniency – five young lives snuffed out in a five-month murder spree that briefly brought terror to the Los Angeles suburbs. The killer thereby earned a place in the 'Worst Ten' category of evil murderers, as judged by forensic psychiatrist Dr Michael Stone.

Born in Pittsburgh on 27 September 1940, Lawrence Sigmund Bittaker was given his name by the couple who adopted him as a baby. The family was constantly on the move as George Bittaker's work in aircraft factories saw him employed at sites in Pennsylvania and then in Florida, Ohio and California. The continual moving had an effect on young Lawrence and a feeling of restlessness and rootlessness set in. Despite a 'genius level' IQ of 138, he dropped out of school when he was 17 after several brushes with police and juvenile authorities, and was thereafter in and out of institutions for two decades.

The crimes he was then accused of seemed mundane. He was arrested for stealing a car, causing a hit-and-run accident and trying to avoid arrest, crimes which resulted in him being given two years' detention at a Californian Youth Authority centre. Within days of his release in August 1959, he was arrested again for car theft and sentenced to another eighteen months at a reform centre in Oklahoma. Again, within only weeks of winning his freedom, he was back in prison for a robbery in Los Angeles.

Bittaker's indeterminate sentence of one to fifteen years was accompanied by obligatory sessions with prison psychiatrists. A report on him by one of them in 1961 is extremely telling. His psychiatric evaluation found him to have 'superior intelligence' but also to be 'manipulative and having considerable concealed hostility'. A hint of the violence that would later erupt came in other psychologists' reports that Bittaker was a 'borderline psychotic', 'basically paranoid' and had a tendency towards 'poor control of impulsive behaviour'. Despite this, he was released within two years.

Just as the doctors had warned, within two months of his release in 1963, Bittaker was back inside on suspicion of robbery. Freed again, a further parole violation had him back in jail in October 1964. His psychiatric records this time around had Bittaker boasting that committing crimes made him feel important – but, disturbingly, he also believed that such acts were not his fault because they were entirely beyond his control. His mental state was clearly labelled 'psychotic'. Yet he was paroled to carry out a further crime spree between modest prison sentences of as short as six months. The most serious offence, stabbing a shop assistant during a theft in 1974, had him behind bars for only four years.

The previous warnings about the dangers of allowing Bittaker back onto the streets were reinforced during this jail term. Prison psychiatrists termed him 'a sophisticated psychopath'. One of them accurately branded him a 'classic sociopath who is incapable of learning to play by the rules', adding: 'Bittaker is a highly dangerous man with no internal controls over his impulses, a man who could kill without hesitation or remorse.' Another judged his prospects for successful parole were 'guarded at best'. Again the warnings were ignored and Bittaker was released in November 1978.

By then, it was too late for the five teenage girls he went on to rape, torture and murder. For Bittaker had now found a satanic soulmate. During his last jail term, in California Men's Colony, San Luis Obispo, he had met up with fellow prisoner Roy Norris. The sick cellmate later explained that the bond that tied them together was the fact that Bittaker had twice saved his life in prison. But there was a further bond – in that both shared a fascination with domination, rape and torture.

Roy Lewis Norris, born in Greeley, Colorado in 1948, was also a school drop-out destined for a life of crime. He joined the Navy and served in Vietnam, but was discharged with psychological problems. He was arrested for attempted rape in San Diego in 1969, and while out on bail was rearrested twice for further sex attacks. Confined in a state hospital as a mentally disordered sex offender, he was freed on probation in 1975. In a sickening parallel with the leniency shown to Bittaker, Norris won his early freedom on the grounds that, according to his release papers, he was someone who would bring 'no further danger to others'. Only three months later he raped a 27-year-old woman and was again jailed – in the same prison as Bittaker.

The pair were released only two months apart and, as arranged, they met up at a seedy hotel in downtown Los Angeles where they rekindled their fantasies and made plans to abduct girls and subject them to sadistic torture. Bittaker bought a cargo van with sliding side doors which, as he explained, made it easy 'to pull up close' to prospective victims 'and open the doors all the way' to snatch them from the streets. He called the vehicle 'Murder Mack' and the two men installed a bed in the back.

From February through to June 1979, Bittaker and Norris cruised up and down the Pacific Coast Highway, stopping at beaches and flirting with girls, many of whom seemed happy enough to pose for photographs – not realising they were being earmarked as potential murder victims. Police later found more than 500 photographs of the smiling females, many of whom were never identified. Bittaker and Norris not only identified their rape and torture targets, they also identified the secret site where they would take their prey: an isolated track in the San Gabriel Mountains, near Glendora. Having found the perfect hideaway, it was time to find the perfect victim.

On Sunday, 24 June, while patrolling the coastline of Greater LA, the pair spotted Cindy Schaeffer, aged 16, walking to her grandmother's house after attending a Christian Youth meeting. When 'Murder Mack' coasted alongside her, she declined the offer of a lift by the two strangers but was bundled into the van, leaving one shoe on the sidewalk. Bound by her wrists and ankles, her cries for help were first drowned out by the van's radio and then stopped with tape bound tightly around her mouth.

In a clinically sickening recollection of the abduction, Bittaker later stated: 'Throughout the whole experience, Cindy displayed a magnificent state of self-control and composed acceptance of the conditions and facts over which she had no control. She shed no tears, offered no resistance and expressed no great concern for her safety. I guess she knew what was coming.'

It is more likely that poor Cindy was in frozen terror as she was driven to the remote hideout. The two men smoked dope and ordered her to strip. Bittaker left the van for an hour to allow Norris time to rape her. When he returned he did the same. Norris was later to say that on his arrival back at 'Murder Mack', Bittaker was trying to strangle Cindy but was bungling it. 'Her body was still jerking and alive to some degree because she was breathing or trying to breathe,' said Norris, who said he finished the job with a wire coat hanger made into a makeshift garrotte. Cindy's body was then tossed into a deep canyon.

On 8 July 1979, another Sunday, 18-year-old hitch-hiker Andrea Hall was thumbing a lift along Pacific Coast Highway. She accepted a ride believing there was only one occupant in the van but, once inside, Norris leaped out from under the bed where he had been hiding. Andrea was bound and taken to the same remote spot, where Norris and Bittaker took turns raping her. Bittaker then dragged the girl outside and took photographs capturing her terror. He stabbed her with an ice pick in both ears and, when she wouldn't die fast enough, strangled her. He then hurled her body over a cliff.

On 3 September, the killers spotted two girls on a bus stop bench. Jackie Gilliam, aged 15 and 13-year-old Leah Lamp accepted an offer from two chatty strangers to join them in smoking a joint on the beach – but panicked when they realised they were being driven in the opposite direction. Once at the secret mountain site, Leah and Jackie were kept alive for two days, during which Norris and Bittaker videotaped their rape and torture ordeal. The recording showed Norris raping Jackie as he demanded she role-play the part of his cousin, a girl at the centre of one of his sexual fantasies. Jackie was finally stabbed in both ears with the ice pick and each man took turns finishing her off by strangulation. Norris then battered Leah with a sledgehammer. The bodies were thrown over a cliff – the ice pick still in Jackie's skull.

On 30 September the evil pair pounced on 16-year-old Shirley Sanders at Manhattan Beach. When Shirley refused a lift, Norris sprayed her in the face with Mace and dragged her into the van. She was raped by both men but incredibly managed to escape. She reported the attack to the police but was in such a distressed state she could recall few details and could not even identify the make of her attackers' vehicle.

Bittaker and Norris were free to kill again. Their last victim was 16-year-old Lynette Ledford, who foolishly was hitching a lift on Halloween Night, 31 October. As real-life spooks, the killers decided against their regular beach haunts and instead joined in the Halloween revellers along the streets of the Sunland and Tijunga district of the San Fernando Valley. Amongst them was Lynette, who happily got into the van, only to be wrestled to the floor and tied up. This time, Norris and Bittaker did not drive to their mountain hideaway but tortured and raped Lynette as they drove around – tape-recording her last moments alive. After strangling her with wire and pliers, they dumped her body on a front lawn in Hermosa Beach, where it was discovered early the next morning.

The murderous couple were apprehended because Norris boasted about the killings to an old prison friend who tipped off the police. Rape victim Shirley Sanders was called in to thumb through police mugshots and was able to pick out Norris and Bittaker. The pair were arrested, and Norris cracked first, blaming Bittaker but confessing to his part in all five killings. Both men were charged with five counts of first-degree murder, kidnapping, robbery, rape, deviant sexual assault and criminal conspiracy. Announcing the charges, Los Angeles police said Bittaker and Norris might be linked to the disappearance of thirty or forty other victims. A stack of 500 photographs of women found in their van included nineteen missing persons, none of whom was ever traced.

Bittaker remained unrepentant but Norris co-operated with police, leading them on a grisly tour of their murder locations. They found the bodies of Leah Lamp and Jackie Gilliam, an ice pick still embedded in her skull, but there was no trace of Andrea Hall or Cindy Schaeffer. To ensure a conviction, the death penalty was reluctantly waived for Norris if he testified against Bittaker. But even while awaiting trial, Bittaker was intent on murder ... He was charged with soliciting two other inmates to kill Shirley Sanders.

Norris turned state's evidence for the three-week trial, which began in March 1981 and made chilling listening for the jurors. What shocked them almost as much as the facts themselves was the defendants' seeming enjoyment of relating what they had done. Talking about the killing of Andrea Hall, Norris said: 'Lawrence told me he was going to kill her. He wanted to see what her argument would be for staying alive.'

The jurors had to listen to the tape recording made of Lynette Ledford's last moments. It contained the sounds of Bittaker slapping her and hitting her with a hammer, all the while shouting: 'Say something girl! Go ahead and scream or I'll make you scream.' Evidence such as this affected the jury members but also caused Deputy District Attorney Steve Kay to break down in tears several times during the course of the trial.

In court, Norris was described as 'compulsive in his need and desire to inflict pain and torture upon women'. But his testimony against his accomplice won him a more lenient sentence: a term of forty-five years to life, with parole possible after thirty years. He ended up in California's Pelican Bay Prison, separated at last from his partner, who was sent to San Quentin.

Bittaker was sentenced to death after the court was told that, if ever released, 'there is little doubt that he would return to a life of crime and possible violence'. The judge imposed an alternate sentence of 199 years, to take effect in the event that his death sentence was ever commuted to life imprisonment. Bittaker was subsequently allowed to launch several appeals, including once after his execution date was fixed for 29 December 1989. On 11 June 1990, the California Supreme Court refused to hear his case again.

Bittaker remained on Death Row, filing litigious claims against the authorities, such as that he had suffered 'cruel punishment' when his lunchtime biscuit arrived broken. He answered fan mail from sick-minded females under his favoured nickname, 'Pliers' Bittaker, referring to how he used pliers to tighten wire coat hangers around his victims' necks.

One man who got an insight into the evil mind of Lawrence Bittaker was Hollywood actor Scott Glenn, who played an FBI profiler in the movie *The Silence of the Lambs*. To prepare for his screen role, he was allowed access to Bittaker's confession tapes. Scott Glenn had felt he would be able to handle what he heard in a bid to acquaint himself with the work of an FBI expert, but instead left the office of real-life profiler John Douglas having been reduced to tears – and expressing himself no longer against the death penalty but in favour of it.

CHAPTER 9

Monster(s) of Florence

Five men wrongly jailed for murders that are still a mystery

Never has a serial killer had a more beautiful and cultured backdrop against which to act out his horrific fantasies. Over a period of seventeen years, the 'Monster of Florence' struck on at least seven occasions in and around the Tuscan city. In each case, a young courting couple were found murdered on or after a dark, cloudy Saturday night in a remote part of the area's lushly rolling hills. In some cases, the female partner would be found spread-eagled on the ground with mutilated genitalia.

Despite the tight location and similar pattern of each murder, Italian police failed miserably in their hunt for the perpetrator. And shamefully, their anxiety to make an arrest, caused by outraged public pressure, resulted in them getting the wrong man – over and over again.

The first murder attributed to the 'Monster of Florence' was in August 1968. Barbara Locci, a 32-year-old married woman, and her lover Antonio Lo Bianco were shot dead as they lay together on the front seat of their car. Barbara's 6-year-old child, who had been asleep in the back of the car, was seized by the killer and carried away. The boy was later found unharmed sobbing on the doorstep of a nearby farmhouse. The farmer called the police, who quickly established the victims' identities and raced to Barbara Locci's home in the town of Lastra a Signa. There, they arrested her husband Stefano who, despite being calmly aware of his wife's string of infidelities, was nevertheless arrested on suspicion of a crime of jealous passion. He was subsequently put on trial and, two years later, was found guilty and sentenced to fourteen years in prison.

It was the first blunder in a catalogue of errors in the law's hunt for the so-called 'Monster of Florence'. After four years of his sentence, Signor Locci's innocence was at last proven and he was released – as a series of similar, merciless killings of courting couples began occurring in the picturesque Tuscany countryside.

The next victims were another courting couple, aged 19 and 18, killed in their car on 14 September 1974. Forensic tests showed the same .22 calibre Beretta pistol had been used as in the first murder. The female victim had been mutilated.

The 'Monster of Florence' did not strike again until 1981. His female victim in June that year was stabbed 300 times. Four months later, another woman was murdered and mutilated.

The 'Monster of Florence' was now killing every year, and all the murders bore the same hallmarks. The men were shot through the driver's window. The same gun was then turned on the girl, whose body was dragged from the vehicle and mutilated with a scalpel. In some cases, though not all, victims had their left breast hacked off. All sixty-seven bullets fired in the sixteen murders were from the same gun and bore the letter 'H'. The monster's last victims were a French couple slaughtered in their tent in 1985. An envelope sent to the Florence public prosecutor contained a piece of flesh cut from the woman's left breast.

In all, five men were wrongly imprisoned during the hunt for the perverted serial killer, and a further suspect named by gossips as the murderer cut his own throat. Three of the wrongly imprisoned men were released when more killings occurred while they were behind bars. A fourth was released by order of a judge because there was no evidence against him. And the fifth is still the subject of fierce debate ...

His name was Pietro Pacciani, a semi-literate peasant farmer who, back in 1951, had been charged with secretly trailing his 16-year-old fiancée and another man into woods. During the course of her seduction, the girl's left breast became exposed – and the stalker could stand the sight no longer. He stormed up to the couple, stabbed the man nineteen times and forced the terrified girl to make love next to the corpse. He served thirteen years in jail for the killing.

The name of Pietro Pacciani re-emerged two decades later as the 'Monster of Florence' paralysed the Tuscany countryside with his reign of bloody terror. As is common in such cases, scores of anonymous notes were sent to police headquarters – and Pacciani's name began cropping up continuously. Detectives speculated that, embittered by the betrayal of his girlfriend, Pacciani had sought to avenge himself on other couples.

Since his release from prison after serving his original murder sentence, Pacciani had married and settled down to raise a family. However, he had again been briefly jailed in 1987 for a violent attack on his wife and for the molestation of his two daughters. Since then, he had become involved in an occult group suspected of performing black masses using female body parts. Pacciani's other hobbies were hunting and taxidermy.

A profile of the unsavoury farmer, now aged 68, was fed into a computer along with more than 100,000 people who had had the opportunity to carry out the crimes. The name-crunching machine whittled it down to one: Pacciani. Police were convinced the monster had been snared but they had only the flimsiest of evidence.

Pacciani's smallholding was taken apart minutely but nothing was found – until a bullet was spotted in a freshly excavated hole. It conveniently matched the other sixty-seven bullets fired in the sixteen murders. It seemed too good to be true. Had a wily policeman planted the evidence? Even in the absence of the murder weapon, a jury was convinced of Pacciani's guilt and, after a six-month trial in 1994, he was convicted of seven of the eight double killings and was jailed for life. A judicial review later tested the evidence and found it wanting, and in February 1996 his conviction was overturned and 71-year-old Pacciani again walked free.

But a new theory had emerged that meant he was not off the hook. It was that there had been not one but three killers. The result was that, just hours after Pacciani's release, two of his friends were arrested on suspicion of involvement in the murders. They were Mario Vanni, 70, and Giancarlo Lotti, 54, supposedly fellow exponents of the satanic arts.

Put on trial in May 1997 accused of five of the double murders, Vanni and Lotti were sentenced to life and twenty-six years respectively. Pacciani, again implicated, faced a new trial – but died in mysterious circumstances before he could face his accusers. In February 1998, he was found on the floor of his home with his face disfigured and his trousers around his ankles. Police attributed his death to a heart attack but this was immediately put in doubt when a post mortem revealed that he had taken – or had been administered – an overdose of a cocktail of drugs.

An investigating magistrate caused further sensation when he voiced the theory that Pacciani had been silenced before he could reveal the identity of the real 'Monster (or more likely Monsters) of Florence'. This sparked conspiracy theories galore that the occult-related murders had been carried out by seemingly respectable, well-connected Florentine citizens.

Despite the longest manhunt in Italian history, despite a number of trials, and following the acquittal of yet another suspect in 2008, the case of the 'Monster of Florence' remained open. One reason that the mystery of the serial killer's identity continued to grip the public imagination so many years after the original crimes is due to a visit to the city during the 1994 trial of Pietro Pacciani by a novelist seeking inspiration for his next work. He was Thomas Harris, author of *The Silence of the Lambs*, who decided that for a further sequel, *Hannibal*, he would move his anti-hero, the cannibal Hannibal Lecter, to the home of the Renaissance and that cradle of civilisation, the idyllic Florence.

Chapter 10

Herman Mudgett, aka H.H. Holmes

'America's first serial killer' could have claimed 200 victims

Herman Webster Mudgett is generally recognised as being America's first identified serial killer. It is a label of infamy that is often disputed, since the 'minimum' number of victims for a murderer to be so classified under the FBI definition is just three. In Mudgett's case, however, there is no doubt – for his tally was anything between 150 and 200.

Born in 1860 into a well-to-do family in Gilmanton, New Hampshire, Mudgett was a natural charmer. The moustachioed lothario was suave, handsome and intelligent. Ejected from medical school for stealing cadavers, with which he planned to defraud insurance companies, his knowledge of medicine nevertheless enabled him to pass himself off as a qualified physician, changing his name to the more distinguished 'Dr Henry Howard Holmes'.

Then he hit the 'Windy City'. He arrived in Chicago in 1886 with two wives, no money, a fake university degree and a determination: to make his fortune by whatever means possible.

As the nineteenth century drew to a close, Chicago was fast growing into a truly great city. It had won the right to stage the coveted World's Fair in 1893 and the years leading up to that momentous event saw new trade and wealth pour in. Prosperity, however, brought with it an army of thieves, swindlers, hoodlums and racketeers, establishing a tradition of crime which the city has to this day cause to regret. Hitherto respectable neighbourhoods were infested with small-time chisellers carving crafty fortunes before making a swift exit. Mudgett fitted in perfectly.

The 26-year-old newcomer to town found it the ideal environment. 'Dr Holmes', as he will be referred to from hereon, realised that Chicago was not only attracting male fortune-seekers but also many eager young women keen to make their names, find fame, fortune and fine husbands. Since Holmes had manners, style, wit and a way about him that women found irresistible, he found them easy prey to his charms.

But first he needed a respectable 'front'. Using a certificate showing him to be a graduate of the prestigious Ann Arbor Medical School in Michigan, he quickly found a job as a pre-scription clerk at a drugstore on the junction of 63rd and South Wallace Streets in the district of Englewood. His employer was a widow, Mrs E.S. Holton, whose husband was suffering from a terminal disease. Nothing could have suited Holmes better.

Mrs Holton found her new hiring wise, charming, courteous and forever helpful to her many customers. Indeed, business had never flourished so much. Mrs. Holton, clearly delighted with her learned employee, took a back seat in the business to care for her bedridden husband in their private quarters above the pharmacy. When he died shortly afterwards, Holmes offered to buy a controlling interest in the business. Mrs Holton readily agreed to the sale but when Holmes defaulted on his payments, she threatened to take him to court. Before she could carry out her threat, however, the widow and her young daughter both disappeared.

Holmes fended off customers' curiosity by telling them that his former boss and her child had moved to California. Mrs. Holton and her daughter were never seen again. Meanwhile, from his newly-acquired base, Holmes launched a series of dis-reputable ventures. He bottled tap water as an all-purpose 'miracle cure'. He sold a 'sure-fire cure for alcoholism' at $50 a bottle. And he claimed to have invented a device for turning water into domestic gas that won him a research contract from a utility company.

As the money rolled in, the 'good doctor' purchased a large double plot of land across the road at 701 and 703 63rd Street. It was to be the site of what later became infamously known as Holmes Castle, a complex three-storey edifice of 100 rooms, with secret passageways, false walls and mysterious trapdoors.

Holmes Castle was speedily erected, via a series of elaborate frauds, bogus deeds and false promises to builders. By 1888, the 28-year-old conman had completed the mysterious structure. Its purpose would not be revealed for another six years – during which time he lured scores of young women to Holmes Castle with the promise of non-existent jobs, working on sundry spurious projects masterminded by their boss. Few of them, it appeared, had ever left – for he would trap his visitors within his labyrinthine mansion. In the Holmes's huge bedchamber was an electric bell which rang whenever a door was opened, so that he knew the movements of his prisoners at any time.

He eventually put paid to the unfortunate victims by leaving them in one of several sealed rooms. These were his gas chambers. In the rooms were mysterious pipes with fake valves, so that 'guests' had no way of stopping the poisonous fumes which eventually took their lives. He would then dispose of the bodies in one of two ways – either in his six-foot wide stove or in barrels of acid.

Holmes was a prolific killer but also an extremely hardworking conman. He found time to travel around America's Midwest perpetrating a string of lucrative frauds. Then a single act of greed caused his downfall. On his regular journeys out of town, Holmes had befriended a small-time Philadelphia hoodlum, Benjamin Pitezel, whom he employed as a part-time accomplice. The pair hatched a plot to fake Pitezel's death by murdering a vagrant, disfiguring the body and then cashing in on a $1,000 insurance policy in Pitezel's name.

All Holmes needed to complete the plan was a crooked lawyer who would supposedly act on behalf of the Pitezel family to collect the loot. By chance, while Holmes was being temporarily held in a Philadelphia jail pending an unrelated fraud investigation, he met up with a long-term prisoner, a notorious bank robber named Marion Hedgepeth who introduced the fraudster to his own crooked lawyer for a share of the booty.

And as far as Hedgepeth knew, everything went according to plan. However, when a body was found on Callowhill Street, Philadelphia, on 3 September 1894, it was not that of a vagrant but of Pitezel himself – murdered by his double-crossing partner in crime. Holmes might have got away with it but for two hitches. The first was that when Hedgepeth realised that he was going to be cheated out of his share of the money, he went to the authorities with the story. The second hitch occurred when Holmes duly lodged the claim, as he had planned – but a sharp-eyed investigator at the insurers' office cast doubt on the scam.

By now, not only was Pitezel dead but so were three of his children, who had been privy to the original plot. Pitezel's wife was also about to follow her family to the grave, but before Holmes could silence her too, the net closed in on the mass murderer. Detectives visited the address to where the money was to have been sent: Holmes Castle. What they discovered there defied belief . . .

They were at first puzzled by the contrast between the ordinary, elegant bedrooms, alongside windowless rooms fed by gas pipes. It took a while for them to realise that the former were used for seduction and the latter were execution chambers. One of these chambers was lined with asbestos, and police could explain its purpose only by speculating that the murderer had devised a means of introducing fire, so that the gas pipe became a blowtorch. In Holmes's office was a giant, 6-foot wide stove, in the grate of which lay part of a bone and a human rib. The basement contained a medieval-style torture rack, and several women's skeletons from which the flesh had been carefully stripped.

A contemporary report of the Chicago Police Department findings within Holmes Castle reads: 'The second floor contained thirty-five rooms. Half a dozen were fitted up as ordinary sleeping chambers and there were indications that they had been occupied by various women who worked for the monster, or to whom he had made love while awaiting an opportunity to kill them.

'Several of the other rooms were without windows and could be made airtight by closing the doors. One was completely filled by a huge safe, almost large enough for a bank vault, into which a gas pipe had been introduced. Another was lined with sheet iron covered by asbestos and showed traces of fire. Some had been soundproofed while others had extremely low ceilings and trapdoors in the floors from which ladders led to smaller rooms beneath.

'In all of the rooms were gas pipes with cut-off valves. But the valves were fakes. The flow of gas was actually controlled by a series of cut-offs concealed in the closet of Holmes's bedroom. Apparently, one of his favourite methods of murder was to lock a victim in one of the rooms and then turn on the gas. Police believed that in the asbestos-lined chamber he had devised a means of introducing fire, so that the gas pipe became a terrible blowtorch from which there was no escape.'

After murdering a victim, Holmes then had the problem of disposing of the body. The grizzly evidence of how he did so was found in the basement. Scattered or buried there were human bones, among them the ribs and pelvis of a child aged no more than 14. A huge barrel contained acid, alongside a surgical table on which lay a box of knives. Underneath the table were several women's skeletons. One macabre theory was that Holmes first acid-burned off the flesh of his victims, then sold the skeletons for medical research.

A nearby storeroom revealed a blood-spattered noose, beneath which were two brick vaults filled with quicklime. Also in the basement was a medieval-style torture rack on which, it was alleged, Holmes tested his sick belief that a human body could be stretched to twice its normal length.

Holmes was not in Chicago when his mansion was raided. He went on the run but was traced to Boston, where he was arrested in November 1894, planning to flee the country along with his third wife. The manhunt for the monster had already made headlines across the continent, at the same time as newspapers in England were writing of the horrific slayings by Jack the Ripper in the heart of London's East End. The Ripper was never caught, but society did get its revenge on the Chicago Monster.

He was put on trial in October 1895 only for the murder of the petty criminal Benjamin Pitezel, although by then it was known that he had also killed the man's three children. The case itself bordered on the farcical because of a dispute between police in Philadelphia and in Chicago over who should try him first. Philadelphia won. Still demanding to be addressed by his alias H.H. Holmes, he vehemently protested his innocence throughout the six-day trial. The twelve-man jury was not fooled and on 2 November, 1895 they returned a verdict of 'guilty in the first degree' to the charge of murdering Pitezel.

After his conviction but while awaiting sentence, Holmes, a wheeler-dealer to the end, sold his story for $7,500 to newspaper tycoon William Randolph Hearst, in which he confessed to twenty-seven murders and six attempted murders in Chicago, Indianapolis and Toronto. It was certainly an underestimation. Although no final count could ever have been made, for much of the evidence had long since been disposed of, police believed that Holmes had murdered no fewer than 150 people and possibly as many as 200, mainly young girls. In addition, the bogus doctor killed at least two of the three wives he bigamously led up the aisle, their deaths being preceded by a horrific period of torture.

Holmes never received the Hearst newspapers' bounty. Thursday, 7 May 1896, was the last day on earth of the arch liar, cheat, conman and the worst serial killer the world had known – justifiably earning a listing in the *Guinness Book of Records* as 'the most prolific murderer in recent criminal history'. Two warders led him from his cell on Death Row of Philadelphia's Moyamensing Prison and onto the gallows. 'Ready, Dr Holmes?' the hooded hangman asked him. 'Yes,' he replied, adding the instruction: 'Don't bungle.' The monster's final instruction was not followed as he would have wished. It took an agonising fifteen minutes before Herman Webster Mudgett, aka Dr H.H. Holmes, died dangling at the end of the hangman's noose.

Chapter 11

Sante & Kenny Kimes

Mother and son 'grifters' were partners in countless crimes

Sante Kimes and her son Kenny Jr did not notch up a high murder count – at least not officially – yet they are placed high on the list of 'World's Most Evil' by forensic psychiatrist Dr Michael Stone. The reason becomes clear when one examines the calculating nature of their crimes. They achieved notoriety for the single slaying of a rich New York widow in 1998, yet their catalogue of criminality goes back a lifetime.

Born Sante Louise Singhrs in Oklahoma City on 24 July 1934, to an Irish mother and Indian father, Kimes was abandoned when the family moved to California. Her father deserted them and her mother became a prostitute, their four children ending up in foster homes and orphanages. Spending most of her days roaming the streets of Los Angeles, Sante was arrested for stealing food when only 9 years old. Reports from that time suggest she had already been sexually abused.

Sante was adopted by her married sister and she attended high school, with reasonable success. But she was still making forays into shopping centres to steal, and used her stepfather's credit cards to obtain goods. In her late teens and twenties, she was strikingly attractive: an attribute she used to good effect, with a string of lovers and two marriages, one of which produced a son. But she was also working as a prostitute and launching herself on a lifelong career of confidence trickery and fraud.

Despite a string of arrests for theft and forgery, in 1971 she met, managed to ensnare and eventually marry wealthy hotel and motel developer Kenneth Kimes, seventeen years her senior. He was worth around $10 million, and Sante spent his money as if there was no tomorrow. She wore beautiful clothes and expensive jewellery and behaved as if she was a Hollywood star. In fact, she was flattered to be told that she looked like Elizabeth Taylor. Despite her husband's wealth, however, Sante could not conquer her compulsion to steal; she later said that she didn't need the money but she continued thieving 'for the thrill'.

The couple had a son, Kenneth Kareem Kimes (latterly known as Kenny Jr), who was 4 years old when his mother was arrested for stealing a fur coat in a top Washington hotel. Kenneth Kimes Sr was by now an alcoholic and enthusiastically went along with his wife's con-artistry. Sante Kimes introduced him as a diplomat and once gained access to a White House reception during the Ford administration. She also used her likeness to impersonate Elizabeth Taylor at restaurants and functions.

In 1985, she was arrested for enslaving poor Mexican maids. She would offer homeless illegal immigrants housing and employment, then keep them prisoner by threatening to report them to the authorities if they didn't follow her orders. As a result, her husband spent much of his fortune on lawyers' fees, defending themselves against charges of slavery. Kenneth Kimes Sr plea-bargained his way out of trouble but his wife was jailed for five years. The judge at her trial called her 'greedy, cunning, and cruel'.

Even so, it is likely that Sante Kimes got away with murder at that time. It was later realised that five teenaged Mexican maids had not been seen since they worked for the Kimes family in California, Nevada, Hawaii and Mexico in the early 1980s. Cynthia Montano, a tutor who was hired to teach young Kenny when his family lived in Mexico City in the 1980s, told police that one of her jobs was to travel into the poor area of the city and find teenage girls to work for them. At least eight young women were later lured away and smuggled into the United States. Several told how they were beaten up and held captive. Five simply vanished.

Sante Kimes's long-suffering husband stuck with her after she was released from prison in 1989, but he died in 1994. Sante carried on living the high life until the money started to run out and that, police believed, was when her son became her partner in crime. Kenny was a student at the University of

California in wealthy Santa Barbara for three years but dropped out in 1996 to join his mother's 'family business'.

Kenny was perfect for the task. He was a smooth talker, with blue eyes, slicked-back blond hair and expensive clothes. Under his mother's tutelage, they became the classic ice-cool con-artists. Like the characters in the 1990 film *The Grifters*, starring Angelica Huston and John Cusack, the pair lived 'on the razor's edge of life' – risking everything for a fast buck and always planning the next big 'sting'.

They criss-crossed the country fleecing the wealthy of their possessions and their money by fraud, forgery, arson or outright theft. They stole cars, watches, mink coats, even a motor home. They dreamed up bank frauds and insurance scams – the first of which was to burn down a Las Vegas home for a $400,000 insurance cheque. They tried to get hundreds of thousands of dollars out of plastic surgeon Dr Joseph Graves in San Diego, California, after Kenny claimed he had a nose job which went wrong and Sante said she suffered a head injury after falling from a table. Kenny picked up his first convictions for robbery and assault, in Florida in late 1997. In January 1988, Sante was investigated for suspected arson after her home was burnt down – the third time in fifteen years.

The couple's crime spree took a more sinister turn when not only property but people began disappearing. In California, New York and the Bahamas, suspected killings were linked to the Kimeses. In each case, mother and son met the victims in the twenty-four hours before their death or disappearance. One of their earliest victims is believed to have been a lawyer who conspired with them in an arson fraud but made the mistake of talking about the plot. He joined them on a holiday to South America and was never seen again. The pair are also suspects in the 1995 disappearance of Jacqueline Levitz, the 62-year-old heiress to a multi-million-dollar estate in Mississippi. She has been officially declared dead and is presumed murdered.

On a trip to the Bahamas in 1996, Sante Kimes befriended a 55-year-old banker, Syed Bilal Ahmed, and got him interested in a possible business deal. One night, she and Ahmed had a dinner date in Nassau but he disappeared and was never seen again, his possessions and luggage having mysteriously van-ished from his hotel suite. A police inquiry failed to solve the mystery, though it is now believed that both mother and son drugged Ahmed, drowned him in a bath and dumped his body at sea.

In March 1998, a successful businessman was found shot dead in a dustbin after telling insurance brokers the Kimeses had been terrorising him. David Kazdin, 64, who had known the crooks for twenty years, was shocked when a Florida bank phoned him about a mortgage he had supposedly taken out. He told friends he suspected that Sante had secretly applied for the loan, thinking he would never find out. Kazdin reported to insurance investigators that he was being bullied and abused by the pair. Days later, he was found shot dead, his body stuffed in a bin at Los Angeles Airport.

Sante and her son disappeared, but not for long. They bought an expensive limousine in Salt Lake City, Utah, and then a luxury motor home in Baton Rouge, Louisiana. In each case, the cheque bounced. Many more crimes were committed by the couple as they travelled across the States in the £50,000 motor home.

In June 1998, the pair arrived in New York and carefully chose their next victim from the society pages of the newspapers. Irene Silverman, 82-year-old widow of a wealthy property developer, owned an eight-storey townhouse in Manhattan, part of which she rented out as apartments to rich tenants. Kenneth Kimes took one of them and paid the first month's rent of £4,000 in cash.

The plan was for Sante Kimes to assume the widow's identity and then appropriate ownership of her $7.7 million mansion. But it appears that Mrs Silverman became suspicious and she and Kenny were spotted having an angry shouting match. She was believed to be about to send him packing – but instead she disappeared. No body has been found but police discovered drops of blood outside her house and believed that she may have been bundled into the Kimes's car and taken into New Jersey to be finished off. Notes written by the victim were later found in the Silverman mansion, detailing her suspicions of the new tenant and his mother.

Time was now running out for the pair, however. A sharp-eyed New York cop saw a TV sketch of Mrs Silverman's missing tenant and realised it bore a striking resemblance to a man questioned the previous day for trying to use a dodgy cheque to buy a second-hand car. When Kenny and his mother were arrested on 5 July, they were carrying Mrs Silverman's passport, a Glock 9mm handgun, wigs and documents.

Detectives contacted their counterparts in several states to try to uncover exactly what manipulative Sante and her son had been up to. It was no easy task, because they went under so many names. When living in Hawaii, for instance, Sante used no fewer than twenty-two false identities. But police quickly realised that there was a dark, sinister side to the Kimes's exploits. Everywhere Sante and Kenny had been, people had disappeared. Said a New York detective: 'They are the most ingenious, evil con-artists we have seen in a long time.'

One of those contacted by police was Las Vegas accountant Sherry Meade, who had been the Kimes's bookkeeper in 1993 and 1994. She said her client had been remarkably candid about her compulsion to steal. She told detectives: 'Kimes said to me, "I am a crook – don't trust me." She would tell you that right up front. She thought it was funny. To her, it was like a game of Monopoly. She just liked to do it and when she got away with it, she was happy and excited as a little kid.'

Despite the fact that Irene Silverman's body was never found, in 2000 both Sante, then aged 63, and her 23-year-old son were convicted of murder. A few months into their 100-year sentences, Kenny made an escape attempt by holding a female television reporter hostage for three hours by pressing a pen into her throat. He was eventually subdued. Kenny and his mother were then moved to Los Angeles to stand trial in 2004 for the murder of David Kazdin. Now facing the death penalty, Kenny changed his plea to guilty and implicated his mother in the murder. He also confessed to killing the Bahamian banker, Syed Bilal Ahmed. That earned him and his mother additional life sentences.

CHAPTER 12

Graham Young

Poisoner watched as family and friends writhed in agony

The cold calculating eyes of Graham Young looked scornfully down at a world he didn't like and didn't want to be part of. He hated the human race and felt no remorse in causing members of it intense pain and final death. He felt he had common cause with his hero, Adolf Hitler, 'a most misunderstood' leader, he believed.

What turned this otherwise undistinguished suburban school-kid into a killer? A tragedy in his childhood would appear to have been, if not the cause, at least the trigger. His mother Bessie developed pleurisy during pregnancy, and died of tuberculosis three months after the birth of her son Graham Frederick on 7 September 1947. The baby was taken from the North London family home and given into the care of his mother's sister, Winnie, with whom he remained for two years before being sent to live with his father, Fred, who had since remarried. After being torn from his first, happy home, the child would never trust anyone's affection again. He grew up yearning for the mother he had never known and hid his pain with an air of eerie coldness.

As a schoolboy, Graham Young demonstrated a sinister bent. He developed a passion for poisons, reading up on infamous villains like the Victorian wife killer Dr William Palmer. Young's father inadvertently encouraged him by buying him a chemistry set. From that moment onwards, instead of climbing trees or playing football, the lonely boy cut himself off from the world and immersed himself in experimentation with dangerous concoctions – and developed a deadly desire to try them out.

At the age of 13, Young read a book that was to change his life and seal his fate: about another Victorian medic, Dr Edward

Pritchard, who poisoned his wife and mother with antimony. Adding four years to his age, Young displayed such an impressive knowledge of toxicology that he was able to convince a local pharmacist that he was 17, and he procured a dangerous quantity of the poisons antimony, digitalis and arsenic and the heavy metal, thallium, for 'study' purposes. He began carrying a phial of the poison around with him at all times, referring to it as 'my little friend'.

Keen to put his knowledge to the test, the most obvious guinea pigs for his bizarre compulsion were his schoolfriends in the London suburb of Neasden. One of them became seriously ill after his sandwiches were laced with antimony over several days. When Young's stepmother discovered the bottle and confiscated it, the murderous prodigy switched to another supplier while turning his attention to members of his immediate family.

In 1961, his elder sister began to suffer severe stomach cramps. Soon bouts of aches and agonising pains afflicted the entire family. His sister was later found to have been poisoned by belladonna but she survived. The following year, in April 1962, his stepmother, Molly, was found by her husband writhing in agony in the back garden of their home, with Young looking on in fascination. She died in hospital and her body was cremated, destroying all evidence of her poisoning. At 14, Young had committed the 'perfect crime'.

Fred Young was next to suffer attacks of vomiting and excruciating cramps, and he was admitted to hospital where he was initially diagnosed with arsenic poisoning. His teenaged son's reaction was not one of sympathy; he was more shocked by the medics' lack of knowledge. 'How ridiculous,' he later sneered, 'not being able to tell the difference between arsenic and antimony poisoning.'

It was Young's chemistry teacher who uncovered the boy's murderous intent. Searching his desk, the teacher found drawings of people dying in agony with bottles of poison by their side. There were also charts of what doses of various poisons would kill a human being. The police were called in and, posing as careers guidance officers, interviewed Young.

He was arrested on 23 May 1962, when police found sachets of antimony tartrate in his pockets. They were also aghast to discover that Young, although admitting affection for his

David Parker Ray drugged and killed his victims in a $100,000 homemade torture chamber he called his 'toy box', which was equipped with what he referred to as his 'friends': whips, chains, pulleys, straps, clamps, leg spreader bars, and surgical blades and saws.

Between 1967 and 1987, Fred West and his wife Rosemary tortured, raped and murdered at least 12 young women and girls, mostly at the couple's home, Number 25 Cromwell Street.

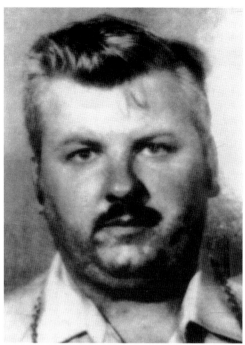

Handsome, suave and deadly, Ted Bundy was one of the most feared serial killers in American history and evaded capture for years.

John Wayne Gacy murdered and dismembered young men he lured to his home. Police found the remains of 29 bodies.

Grinning gun-toting Ivan Milat was a ritual killer who preyed on backpackers in Australia.

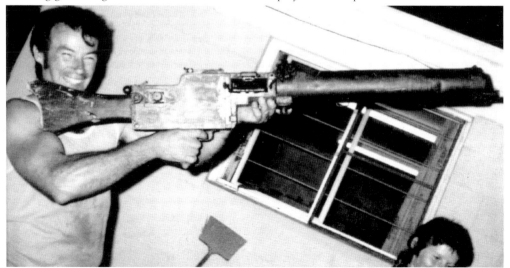

Herman Mudgett gassed many of his victims by forcing them into a trunk in one of the death chambers within his Chicago 'Torture Castle'.

Smirking Lawrence Bittaker facing the death sentence in court in 1981 – first murder trial in California to be televised.

Above: Graham Young poisoned friends, colleagues and family members, displaying neither sympathy nor remorse for their suffering.

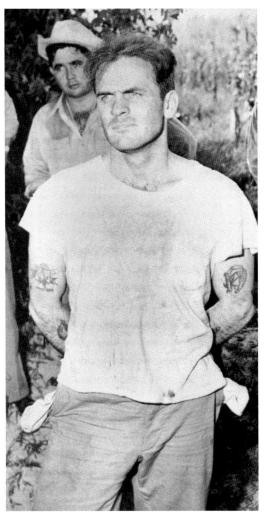

Above: Gerald Gallego is captured after being sniffed out by bloodhounds, so ending a murderous rampage by the sadistic killer and his willing female accomplice.

Kenneth Bianchi, one of a pair of Californian killers, testifies in court against his accomplice Angelo Buono.

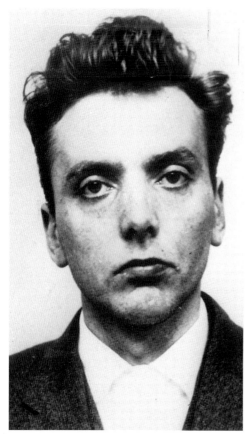

Above left and right: Faces of pure evil … the so-called Moors Murders were carried out by Ian Brady and Myra Hindley between July 1963 and October 1965.

Sadistic mutilator Randy Kraft kept a sick 'score sheet' of his victims. It is believed he killed over 60 people.

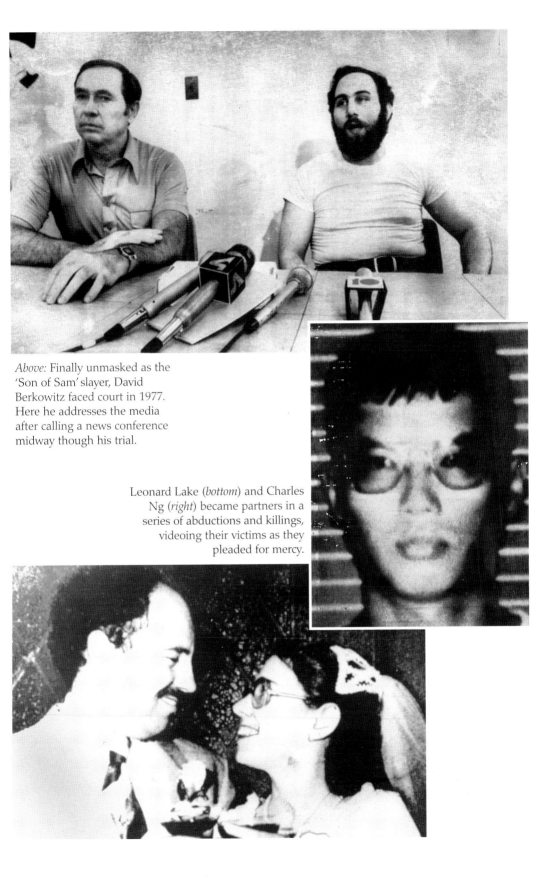

Above: Finally unmasked as the 'Son of Sam' slayer, David Berkowitz faced court in 1977. Here he addresses the media after calling a news conference midway though his trial.

Leonard Lake (*bottom*) and Charles Ng (*right*) became partners in a series of abductions and killings, videoing their victims as they pleaded for mercy.

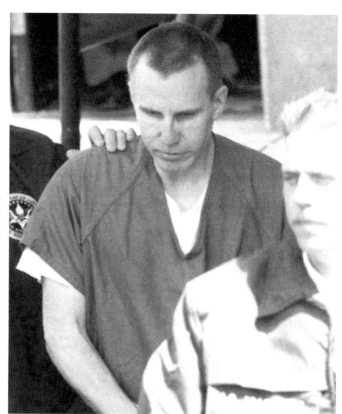

Joseph Swango was convicted of murdering four patients in his care. Estimates put his number of victims at over 100.

Nurses laughed and joked about disposing of patients in their care. Brought to trial in Vienna, they were (left to right): Stefanija Meyer, Irene Leidolf, Maria Gruber and Waltraud Wagner.

family, was far more concerned with the outcome of his experiments than with their welfare. Sessions with a police psychiatrist confirmed that he was a serial killer in the making but, although he admitted the poisoning of his father, sister and schoolfriend Williams, no murder charges could be brought against him because his stepmother's cremation had destroyed the evidence.

Brought to trial, the juvenile poisoner was found guilty but insane. Still only 15, he was committed to Broadmoor maximum-security hospital, the youngest inmate since 1885, for a minimum period of fifteen years.

Within weeks, a fellow inmate died of poisoning by cyanide, which Young claimed to have extracted from laurel bush leaves. The killer was not taken seriously and the death was recorded as 'suicide'. Another record on his file shows that in 1970, when recommended for early release, he told a psychiatric nurse that he planned to kill one person for every year he had been in Broadmoor.

His incarceration fell well short of the 'fifteen years minimum' that the judge had ordered. After nine years, Young, apparently now cured of his fatal fascination, was released. In June 1971, he applied for a menial job at the firm of John Hadland, makers of specialist, high-speed optical and photographic instruments in Bovingdon, Hertfordshire. While admitting to knowing something about chemicals, he did not confess his guilty past. Instead, he told how he had suffered a mental breakdown after the death of his mother. A psychiatrist's report produced on his behalf stated that Young had made 'an extremely full recovery' from a 'deep-going personality disorder'. Young would 'fit in well and not draw any attention to himself in any community', the report added. Young did slot in. His workmates made him welcome in his capacity as storeman. They shared jokes and cigarettes with him. In return, he became unofficial tea boy, happily furnishing them with hot drinks to repay their kindness.

Within weeks of Young joining the firm, staff began to be struck down with a mystery disease, which they nicknamed 'the Bovingdon bug'. Seventy of the staff were affected, with symptoms including diarrhoea, cramps, backache, nausea and numbness. Head storeman Bob Egle, 59, one of Young's closest colleagues, was among the worst hit. After eight days of searing pain, he died in hospital. The doctors blamed broncho-pneumonia and polyneuritis.

Meanwhile, other employees were still wracked with pain. By September, 60-year-old Fred Biggs was ill. His condition deteriorated over the weeks and, in November, he died. Young seemed genuinely shocked and saddened by the death of Egle. He even went to his victim's funeral. And of Biggs's demise, he later commented: 'Poor old Fred. I wonder what went wrong? He shouldn't have died. I was very fond of old Fred.'

Meanwhile, other workers were falling sick by the score and there was a wave of panic in the company. Employees feared the chemicals they were using would cause them permanent damage. An investigation by the management included face-to-face interviews between the head of the inquiry, Dr Arthur Anderson, and each member of the workforce.

Young's arrogance was now his undoing. During his inter-view, Young could not resist revealing the impressive extent of his expert knowledge. The humble storeman asked the doctor whether he believed the illnesses were consistent with signs of thallium poisoning. Dr Anderson was instantly suspicious. Young's knowledge of chemicals appeared too detailed for a layman. He wanted to find out more about the background of the young man who had been employed at Hadland just six months before.

The local police force was called in, who in turn contacted Scotland Yard. Within hours, the full, sorry story of Young's miserable past caught up with him. He was arrested on sus-picion of murder. Young was arrested on 21 November 1971, in Sheerness, Kent, where he had been visiting his father. He was carrying a bottle of thallium – tasteless, odourless and deadly. Young freely admitted his involvement, unable to let the opportunity to prove his skills pass. 'I could have killed them all if I wished,' he told detectives, 'but I let them live.' At his home, police found rows of bottles containing a variety of chemicals. They were stacked beneath the picture portraits of Young's heroes, Hitler and other members of the Nazi high command.

At his trial, which began on 19 June 1972 at St Albans Crown Court, Young was accused of two murders, two attempted murders and two cases of administering poison. Despite his earlier verbal confession to police, he denied the charges, seemingly relishing his moment of notoriety in the dock. He remained cool and aloof, his only upset being that the press had labelled him 'The Teacup Poisoner'; Young believed that 'World Poisoner' would better fit his infamy.

His arrogance in court was overwhelming. The case appeared clear cut, and a single entry in his diary, relating to the death of one of his work colleagues, Biggs, should, on its own, have sealed his fate: 'I have administered a fatal dose of the special compound to F. and anticipate a report on his progress on Monday. I gave him three separate doses.' However, when this and other incriminating diary entries were produced, Young claimed they were no more than notes for the plot of a novel.

On 29 June, the jury took less than an hour to find Graham Young guilty, and he was given four life sentences. He did indeed spend the remainder of his miserable life in custody. In August 1990, warders at Parkhurst Prison found 42-year-old Young dead of a heart attack on the floor of his cell.

CHAPTER 13

Angelo Buono & Kenneth Bianchi

Mysterious 'Hillside Stranglers' were vicious cousins in crime

When Judge Ronald George reluctantly committed Angelo Buono to serve the rest of his natural life in prison, it was clear from his closing comments that he considered the death penalty the only punishment fitting for this vicious and perverted murderer. The judge's hands were tied because of the jury's surprise recommendation for a life sentence. Judge George showed his disapproval when, on 31 October 1983, he told the court: 'Angelo Buono and (his accomplice) Kenneth Bianchi subjected various of their murder victims to the administration of lethal gas, electrocution, strangulation by rope, and lethal hypodermic injection. Yet the two defendants are destined to spend their lives in prison, housed, fed and clothed at taxpayer expense, better cared for than some of the destitute law-abiding members of our community.'

Cousins Buono and Bianchi had more than family in common. They both nurtured fantasies of violent rape and murder, each experimenting through their young adulthood with sexual perversions so that, despite their sixteen-year difference in ages, they formed a deadly duo after Bianchi moved in with his older cousin in 1977. Together they embarked on a killing spree that lasted for two years and resulted in the murders of twelve young women.

Kenneth Bianchi was a troubled youth. Born to an alcoholic prostitute on 22 May 1951, in Rochester, New York State, Kenneth was raised from birth by foster parents. His foster mother, Mrs Frances Bianchi, worried about her son's tempers and habitual lying, commenting that he 'had risen from the cradle dissembling'. Following her husband's death, Frances had to go out to work, leaving young Kenneth to fend for himself. He went to college, but soon dropped out, finding work as a security guard but also indulging in petty crime. He would give trinkets he had stolen to girlfriends in an attempt to win their affection. In 1971, he wed his high-school sweetheart but the marriage lasted only eight months before she left him.

Continuing with his life of petty crime, Bianchi drifted across the US over the next few years until he settled in the greater Los Angeles area and teamed up with his cousin, Angelo Buono, eventually moving in with him in his house at 703 East Colorado Street, Glendale, in the San Fernando Valley. Although an ugly brute of a man, both physically and mentally, cousin Angelo Buono was very popular with women and gloried in the nickname 'Italian Stallion'. He married several times and fathered children both in and out of wedlock.

Born in Rochester, New York State, on 5 October 1934, Angelo Buono's divorced mother Jenny moved to California in 1939 and struggled to raise her son with good family and religious values. However, the young Angelo seemed to have a desperate need for sex, boasting to friends about raping and sodomising girls even at the young age of 14. He appeared to have a loathing for women and a desire to hurt and humiliate them, including his mother and sister.

Buono's criminal record began with petty theft in adolescence. He was sent to the Paso Robles School for Boys after an auto theft conviction. Shortly after his release, he married his pregnant girlfriend, Geraldine Vinal, only to walk out on her a week later. She gave birth to his first son in 1956 while Angelo was again in custody for thieving. His second wife, Mary Castillo, had already borne him a second son in 1956 before the couple were married. They continued to produce children every year or two until Mary filed for divorce in 1964, citing his violence and perverse sexual demands. She had given birth to five children during their marriage and struggled to feed them, relying on state welfare until, desperate for money, she tried to reconcile her differences with Buono, pleading with him for a reconciliation. His response was to handcuff her and threaten to kill her with a gun pressed into her stomach.

Buono started his own car upholstery business and worked from home. By 1975, he had built up a reasonable trade and had enough spare money to enjoy a bachelor life. He had an inexplicable sexual magnetism and, by the time his cousin moved in, he had surrounded himself with a virtual harem of young girls, seemingly willing to pander to his perverted sexual demands. The younger Bianchi was soon enjoying this depraved lifestyle, often bringing prostitutes back to East Colorado Street to share with his cousin.

Two such prostitutes became the first victims of the killing cousins. The body of 21-year-old Hollywood hooker Elissa Kastin was found on 6 October 1977, on a hillside on Chevy Chase Drive. She had been violently raped before her murder. Twelve days later, the naked body of their second victim was found spreadeagled near the Forest Lawn Cemetery. Nineteen-year-old Yolanda Washington had been raped and then strangled. She had been tightly bound at the wrists and ankles and rope marks could still be seen around her neck. This time, the killers had cleaned the corpse thoroughly so that no evidence could be traced back to them.

Police at this point believed that they were hunting for a prostitute-hating pervert. It was only the discovery of 15-year-old Judith Miller on 31 October that convinced them that two men had been involved. Judith's murder bore all the trademarks of the earlier deaths: she had been viciously raped then strangled and left on a hillside in Glendale. But the cousins had been careless with their clean-up operation – and two sets of sperm samples were taken from the body.

With the discovery of more murder victims, a pattern emerged. The girls were all raped and sometimes sodomised before murder. The favoured means of murder was strangulation, but the killing cousins also experimented with other methods, including lethal injections, electric shocks and carbon monoxide poisoning. The bodies were cleaned to avoid leaving any clues and were left strategically placed on hillsides where they would be easily found – often arranged in bizarre and lascivious poses.

The media named the killers 'The Hillside Stranglers' and Los Angeles became gripped with fear. The sale of guns soared and parents kept a careful watch on their children, refusing to let them out after dark. For the Hillside Stranglers were no longer killing only prostitutes; they were now targetting middle-class children, abducted from their homes and neighbour-hoods.

The Los Angeles Police Department came under enormous pressure to solve the case and bring the murderers to justice but the cousins, although blatant in their modus operandi, remained undetected. They would cruise the streets of Los Angeles in Buono's car, using fake police badges to lure un-suspecting girls into their 'unmarked police vehicle'. They would then take them back to the privacy of Buono's home where they would abuse and torture their young victims before killing and disposing of them.

The pace of the murders accelerated. In one single week in November 1977, five bodies of murdered girls were discovered. Twelve-year-old Dolores Cepeda and 14-year-old Sonja Johnson had been missing from St Ignatius School for a week before their corpses were found in Elysian Park. They had last been seen getting off a bus together and talking to two men in a large two-tone sedan car. The same night, the body of 20-year-old honours student Kristina Weckler was found on a hillside in Highland Park. The next discovery left hardened cops in tears. The badly decomposed body of Jane King was uncovered on an exit ramp of the Golden State Freeway. The 28-year-old had been a stunning girl with model looks and figure.

The very next day, Thanksgiving, the body of Lauren Wagner was found. The 18-year-old student lived at home in the San Fernando Valley and had been snatched from her own driveway. The door of her car hanging open alerted her dis-traught father to the abduction, which was seen by a neighbour. The witness told police that her dog had been disturbed by what she took to be an argument between Lauren and two men. As she was bundled into their two-tone car, Lauren had cried out: 'You won't get away with this.' The witness was able to provide a good description of Bianchi and Buono – the younger one tall with acne scars, the older one short, Latin-looking with bushy hair.

On 14 December 1977, the body of Kimberley Martin was found. The pace of the killings then briefly slackened, but on 17 February 1978, the body of Cindy Hudspeth was discovered in the boot of a car. Both were naked, raped, strangled and fastidiously cleaned.

Then, to the bafflement of detectives, the killings stopped. With no further significant leads, the special 'Hillside Stranglers' murder squad that had been set up was disbanded. But the reason the killings had ceased was simply that Bianchi had moved away. He had become sickened, not with his and Buono's activities, but with the filthy conditions at his house.

Bianchi was now settled in Bellingham, Washington State, where he had moved in with his long-term girlfriend, Kelli Boyd, and their baby son. Astonishingly, he applied for a position with the local police force but ended up working as a security guard. It was not long, however, before he was compelled to kill again – but without his partner in crime, he made a series of blunders that eventually led to his capture and the subsequent arrest of Buono.

In January 1979, Bianchi lured two students, Diane Wilder and Karen Mandic, to a luxury residence in Bellingham that his security firm had on its books. He promised them an easy job house-sitting, and they eagerly agreed. Shortly afterwards, their bodies were found in the back of a car. The trail led straight to Bianchi, for the girls had boasted to their friends of their 'good fortune' and had described their 'benefactor', the security guard. Bianchi had also been careless with his cleaning, and several bloodstained items of clothing were found hidden at his home. Under interrogation, Bianchi let slip links to the series of unsolved murders in Los Angeles, and cousin Buono was also arrested.

At his trial for the two Bellingham murders, Bianchi pleaded insanity, claiming that he suffered from 'multi personality disorder'. He managed to persuade six Washington State psychiatrists into supporting his plea, thereby saving him from the death penalty in Washington, where he would have faced hanging.

The inadmissibility of 'insane' Bianchi's testimony delayed the start of Buono's trial until November 1981. It was to last for two years and involved 400 witnesses. Among the most important of these was 27-year-old Catherine Lorre, daughter of the actor Peter Lorre. She recalled the night she was stopped by Bianchi and Buono, pretending to be police officers. She had shown them her identification papers, which included a photograph of her with her famous father – and that, it is believed, saved her life. The photo discouraged the killers from abducting a celebrity's daughter, for fear of intensifying the manhunt.

Throughout the prolonged trial, Buono consistently denied all charges and blamed the slayings on his cousin. Indeed, there was very little forensic evidence, so thorough had been the clean-up at his house. Detectives failed to find a single fingerprint of the victims, nor even one of Buono himself. However, fibres from a chair were matched with those found on one of the victims' bodies, and a single eyelash from one of the girls was also identified at the property. The trial ended in November 1983 with Buono being found guilty of two of the murders. Under California law at that time, as a 'multiple murderer' he faced either execution or life in prison without the possibility of parole. Buono took the stand to appeal to the jury that his 'moral and constitutional rights have been broken' and – to the judge's obvious dismay – the jurors deliberated for an hour before sparing him the death penalty.

Angelo Buono was initially sent to Folsom Prison where he married Christine Kizuka, a supervisor at the Los Angeles state Employment Development Department. He was later transferred to Calipatria State Prison where he died at the age of 67 on 21 September 2002, of a suspected heart attack. Meanwhile, his erstwhile partner Kenneth Bianchi languished in Washington's Walla Walla prison where, with a life sentence, he had time to reflect on Judge Ronald George's parting shot at the evil duo: 'I am sure, Mr Buono and Mr Bianchi, that you will only get your thrills by reliving over and over the tortures and murders of your victims, being incapable as I believe you to be of ever feeling any remorse.'

CHAPTER 14

Theresa Knorr

Mother who ordered her sons to burn their sister alive

It was watching an episode of *America's Most Wanted* that finally gave Terry Knorr the courage to contact the police and tell them the horrific story that had been haunting her for eight years . . . her sisters' murders at the hands of her own mother. Terry described to detectives how her mother had first shot and later burned alive her daughter Suesan in 1984 and beaten and starved her eldest daughter Sheila to death in 1985, disposing of her decomposing body wrapped in blankets in a home-made casket. The police were then able to make a connection with the unsolved cases surrounding two 'Jane Doe' bodies, and Theresa Knorr was finally apprehended for their murders.

Theresa Jimmie Francine Cross was born on 12 March 1946, in Sacramento, California. The youngest of Jim and Swannie Cross's four children, Theresa was her mother's favourite and she enjoyed a happy childhood until her father was diagnosed with Parkinson's disease in the late 1950s and had to leave his job. He became depressed and often took his frustrations out on his children. When Theresa's beloved mother died suddenly of heart disease in March 1961, Theresa was bereft and felt that she had lost all security she had ever known. Not surprisingly, she latched onto the first boy to show her any affection and, aged 16, she married Clifford Clyde Sanders in September 1962.

Their marriage very quickly began to go downhill. Theresa was insecure and possessive, often accusing Clifford of infidelities. He would leave her in their small apartment and go out drinking with friends, wasting money they could ill afford as, in July 1963, Theresa gave birth to their first son, Howard, and shortly after became pregnant again, making it necessary to move house. Theresa and Clifford often quarrelled, and in June 1964 she filed an assault-and-battery charge against him following a particularly violent argument. She later dropped the charges and normal family life resumed. However, in July 1964, Clifford finally had enough of her nagging and packed his bags to leave. She shot him dead but was subsequently acquitted of his murder after claiming self-defence for herself and her unborn child.

Theresa couldn't bear to be alone and very soon moved in with Estelle Thornsberry. He doted on Theresa and her baby daughter Sheila, born in March 1965, but she soon tired of him, using him as a babysitter while she cheated on him with his best friend. When her affair was discovered, she moved out, taking Howard and Sheila and staying with friends until Husband Number Two came along.

Robert Knorr was a private in the Marine Corps. After a spell in Vietnam, where he sustained several injuries, he was shipped home to recuperate. Theresa was already seven months pregnant with Suesan Marline when the couple married in 1966. Suesan's birth was followed in 1967 by William Robert and in 1968 by Robert Wallace.

Robert Knorr's injuries left him unable to continue actively in the Marine Corps and he was given work as a burial escort, which necessitated him travelling across the country at a moment's notice. This did not suit Theresa and soon she was accusing him of being unfaithful, just as she had done with Clifford. She took her anger out on the children, beating them or locking them in a cupboard when they irritated her.

Robert tried to make the marriage work, but in 1970 he could take no more of her cruelty and unpredictability and the couple were divorced. Two months later, Theresa gave birth to her sixth and final child, Theresa Marie, and although Robert attempted to visit the children, she repeatedly refused him access until he eventually gave up.

Her next marriage, to Ronald Pulliam in 1971, lasted for only a year as Theresa again used him for childcare while she went out partying, sometimes staying out all night. Following their divorce, Theresa started to drink heavily. The children grew used to the beatings, abuse and humiliation – their mother referring to them as her 'demon seeds' from Bob Knorr. And the more Theresa Knorr drank, the crueller she became.

In 1976, within just three days of meeting 59-year-old Chet Harris, a copy-desk editor at the *Sacramento Union* newspaper, she married again. It became apparent almost immediately that she had made yet another mistake. His hobbies included mysticism and mythology and, by contrast, taking photographs of nude women. As their relationship floundered, Harris became closer to Suesan than to his wife, and this led to Suesan becoming the main target for Theresa's anger and frustration. When the marriage ended only two months later, her drinking and binge-eating became much worse, she put on weight, disconnected the telephone and forbade the children from bringing home any friends. The family became isolated and at the mercy of their mother's paranoia.

Theresa convinced herself that Suesan was a witch and had put a spell on her to make her gain weight. She even force-fed the girls with macaroni cheese, laced with lard, to make them put on weight. If they vomited, they had to eat that as well. Suesan's life became unbearable. Beatings were commonplace, with her brothers now forced to join in. If they failed to hit her hard enough, they were made to hit again until Theresa was satisfied.

Driven beyond endurance, Suesan ran away from home and was picked up by a truancy officer. She was placed in a psychiatric hospital where she told counsellors all about her tortured home life. But the salvation she sought never came. Theresa persuaded the experts that Suesan suffered from mental problems and she was allowed to take her home – where she suffered one of the most severe beatings of her young life before being handcuffed to her bed.

In 1982, during yet another violent exchange, Theresa pulled out a handgun and shot her daughter in the chest. Too fearful to take her to hospital, Theresa dressed the wound – with the bullet still embedded in her – and incredibly Suesan survived. She was now desperate to escape home, however, and in July 1984, after suffering one last horrific beating, she begged to be let go. Amazingly, Theresa agreed, provided the bullet that was still inside her was removed.

The operation that ensued was horrific. Suesan was drugged and given strong alcohol until she passed out. Then 15-year-old Robert was forced to dig the bullet out of her body with a knife. Not surprisingly, the wound became infected and, despite anti-biotics, she was soon critically ill. When Suesan became delirious, her mother taped her mouth shut to stop her cries and bound her arms and legs. After a few days of watching her daughter's desperate plight, Theresa forced the boys to help her take Suesan out to the car. They drove south out of Sacramento until Theresa was satisfied the spot was secluded enough and then, dousing her with petrol, Theresa threw a lighted match and walked away from her daughter's agonising last moments.

Family life continued in much the same pattern following Suesan's murder, except that Sheila now bore the brunt of Theresa's cruelty. In 1985, she forced the 20-year-old to work as a prostitute to supplement the family's meagre income. Although Sheila hated this, at least it gave her some freedom from the house. It wasn't long, however, before Theresa's paranoia again took hold and she accused her daughter of catching a venereal disease and passing on the infection to her. When Sheila denied this, she was beaten black and blue, tightly bound with duct tape, then locked in a cupboard. The rest of the family were forbidden to go near her and, after just three days, Sheila's cries ceased.

A further three days passed before the children were allowed to remove her body. Their mother wrapped the corpse in blankets, stuffed it into a box and drove to a remote spot where the boys unloaded it from the car and dumped it. When the body was discovered, it was so badly decomposed that the cause of death could not be ascertained, nor the identity, and the body was named a 'Jane Doe'.

Following Sheila's death, the family at last split up in 1986. Howard, then aged 26, William, 24, and Terry, only 16, went their own ways while only 19-year-old Robert remained with his mother when she moved to Las Vegas. There was really little hope for him considering his home life, and in 1991 he shot a barman in a botched burglary and was sentenced to sixteen years in jail.

In 1992 Terry Knorr contacted the police after watching an episode of *America's Most Wanted*. She told them of the two murders and her brothers' involvement in both crimes with her mother. When they had made the connection with the two 'Jane Doe' cases, Theresa was arrested and charged with multiple murder and murder by torture. She initially pleaded not guilty, but on learning that Robert was planning to testify against her to help his case, she changed her plea to guilty in an attempt to avoid the death penalty. She received two consecutive life sentences, Judge William Ridgeway referring to her crimes as 'callousness beyond belief'.

CHAPTER 15

Dennis Rader

'Bind, Torture, Kill' taunt of killer who bragged of his crimes

Outwardly he was a pillar of the community, a church-goer, a scout leader, a respectable family man. In reality, he was a sickening serial killer who managed to evade justice for thirty years. His name was Dennis Rader, but he was better known by his nickname 'BTK' because of his method of murder: Bind, Torture, Kill.

During his long reign of terror in Wichita, Kansas, that left ten dead, he strangled four members of one family, hanged an 11-year-old girl from a sewer pipe to watch her die, photographed the bodies of his victims – one on a church altar – and taunted police by sending them trophies taken from the corpses.

When his murderous spree finally ended in February 2005, relatives of his victims wept at the police press conference announcing his arrest. Wichita's police chief Norman Williams told them: 'This has been a life sentence of heartbreak and pain for you folks. But for me, this is the happiest day of my career.'

Despite the horrific nature of his crimes, to most people who knew him father-of-two Rader had just seemed 'an ordinary guy'. He was an attentive parent who had taken his children, when young, on camping and fishing expeditions. A United States Air Force veteran, he had been a Scout leader for his son Brian's troop, and was skilled at tying knots.

Fellow churchgoers were among those most stunned by his arrest. He helped children gather their crayons before worship started and chatted with them about school. Bob Smyser, who ushered with him at Christ Lutheran Church, said: 'If you named 500 people who were going to be arrested for this, he wouldn't be on the list.'

Rader seemed to live by the book. As an installation manager at the ADT alarm company in the 1980s, he drew intricate, accurate layouts of security systems and homes – not unlike the crime-scene diagrams sketched by BTK which he tauntingly sent to the media.

His overly strict adherence to the thick binder of company rules known as the 'blue pages' rankled with some colleagues and he left the company in 1989. In 1991 he became a so-called 'code-compliance officer' in Park City, the working-class Wichita suburb where he, his wife Paula and one of BTK's victims lived.

It seemed an ideal job for a lover of rules. 'He'd come by and measure your grass, and if it was too long he'd give you a warning and tell you that you had ten days to mow it or get a fine,' said James Reno, who lived a few doors away from the Raders. He would wander through back yards shooting stray pets with a tranquilliser gun. But though local kids made up a game called 'Hide from Dennis', taking cover whenever they saw his white van approach, he seemed a byword for law and order.

Yet Rader had always been a secret sadist, with the classic serial-killer background of torturing small animals. He was later to say that his depravity started in childhood when he saw his grandparents butcher chickens. But his depths of evil did not find full expression until 1974 when, at the age of 28, he developed a lust for 11-year-old Josephine 'Josie' Otero.

Rader assembled what he termed his 'hit kit' – a holdall containing guns, tape, rope and handcuffs – and went to the Oteros' home, cutting the phone line before bursting in on Josie, her 9-year-old brother Joey and parents Joe, 38, and Julie, 34. Trapping them in their bedroom and threatening them with a pistol, he tied them all up, binding their hands and feet and gagging them.

Joe was the first to die. A bag was placed over his head before Rader strangled him with a rope. He attempted to dispose of the screaming Julie in the same way. Young Joe was next but as he watched the choking youngster die, Julie came round and begged him not to kill her son. He again turned on her and this time strangled the life from her.

It was the fate of 11-year-old Josie that sent a wave of revulsion through the Kansas town and then throughout the whole of America. Her body was found hanging from the basement sewer pipe. Her hands were bound behind her back and she wore nothing but socks and a jumper. The rest of her clothes were in a pile by the foot of the stairs, left by her killer before he carried out a sex act on her corpse.

His first killing filled him with bloodlust. Still playing the devoted dad and churchgoer, he began a trail of death that would end with ten horrific crimes and see him become one of the country's most notorious and elusive serial killers. And all the while, he kept a secret diary of death, calling his targets 'projects' and dubbing his manhood 'Sparky'.

As police hunted the Oteros' killer, Rader targeted 21-year-old student Kathryn Bright, who returned home with her younger brother Kevin on a warm April afternoon in 1974 to find a man in the house. Wearing a black stocking cap, camouflage jacket and black gloves, he was waiting for them in the front bedroom, gun in hand.

Kevin, who was to be the sole survivor of a BTK attack, related what happened next: 'He told us he was wanted in California and was headed for New York. He said all he wanted was money and a car, and he wouldn't hurt us.'

Rader forced Bright to tie Kathryn to a chair in a back bedroom, then tied him up too and tried to strangle him. 'I just fought and fought,' he said. 'He wasn't expecting me to get loose.'

Rader shot Bright three times in the head. Bright played dead and, once the killer had left, stumbled out and fled. By then, Kathryn had also got free – but Rader caught her and stabbed her eleven times. She did not survive.

Police failed to link her murder to the Oteros' massacre. And the description Kevin Bright provided– average-size, bushy moustache, 'psychotic eyes' – led to nothing at first. This seemed to upset Rader, who wrote to the *Wichita Eagle* newspaper, claiming to be 'BTK', bragging about the slaughter and promising to kill again. Police could now have no doubt about the authenticity of the killer, for the letter contained details of the Otero case that only the murderer could have known.

Wichita was now in the grip of fear and business boomed for security companies. Ironically, Rader landed a job with a burglar alarm firm, allowing him to case his targets' homes. At this period, however, the killing spree stopped for three years as Rader again became the dutiful family man, looking after his wife Paula and their newborn son Brian.

Then BTK returned with a vengeance. In March 1977, Shirley Vian, 24, was found bound and strangled in her Wichita home. After locking her three children in the bathroom, Rader had led her into her bedroom, stripped her and bound her. The terrified woman threw up on the floor, and Rader calmly fetched her some water – before tying a plastic bag over her head and strangling her. He stole her pants as a trophy.

That December, Nancy Fox suffered the same fate. Returning from work, the 25-year-old secretary took off her coat and strolled into her kitchen, where the killer was waiting for her, handcuffs in one hand and strangling belt dangling from the other. Rader handcuffed her and stripped her, before assaulting her from behind. Nancy fought back fiercely, grabbing his testicles and digging her nails in. Rader, who later claimed to have enjoyed the pain, then throttled her until she passed out. When Nancy came round, he whispered in her ear: 'I killed the four people in that family, the Oteros. I killed Shirley Vian. I'm BTK. And you're next.' Then he yanked his belt around her neck and held it until she died.

Desperate for recognition for his crimes, Rader's voice was caught on tape when he used a payphone to report the murder. Early in 1978, he sent letters and cards to local media, claiming responsibility for the murders, including a poem called 'Oh, Death to Nancy'. Still frustrated by a lack of media interest, he wrote to a TV station, asking: 'How many do I have to kill before I get some national attention?'

The following year Anna Williams, 63, received a letter, apparently from BTK, saying he had hidden in her house to kill her but got tired of waiting. Chillingly, the envelope contained one of her scarves.

It would be several years between his seventh victim and his eighth. Police assumed BTK had died but the apparent reason for his going to ground was the birth of Rader's daughter Kerri in June 1978.

In April 1985, however, BTK's urge to kill returned. He murdered Marine Hedge, a 53-year-old neighbour, and took her body to the Christ Lutheran Church where he was congregation president. Rader placed the corpse on the altar and took bondage photos before dumping it in a ditch.

In September 1986, he entered the home of Vicki Wegerle, 28, after posing as a telephone repairman. He strangled her to death and kept her driving license as a trophy.

By now, Wichita was paralysed by fear. Women bought guns and few dared walk the streets alone after dark. But suspicion still did not fall on Dennis Rader, who was now using his son's scout camp as an alibi, sneaking off in the night to carry out the killings.

His final victim was Dolores Davis, 62, strangled in 1991. He abducted her and dumped her body under a bridge – then returned to it later to put a mask over the corpse's head and take photographs of it. As always, he performed a sex act at the scene.

Police failed to link the latest deaths to the earlier BTK murders and the trail may have gone cold if the *Wichita Eagle* had not run an article marking the thirtieth anniversary of the Otero family's slaughter in 2004. Two months later the *Eagle* received a letter containing pictures of Vicki Wegerle's body and a copy of her driving licence. The return address read Bill Thomas Killman.

Police began communicating with the killer through personal ads and in December of that year they received a package from BTK, containing Nancy Fox's driving licence and a doll bound at the hands and feet with a plastic bag over its head. Other macabre mementoes, including a doll symbolising Josie Otero's murder, were left for the police in cereal boxes.

A package sent to Fox TV station KSAS in February 2005 was to be his last. In the envelope was a floppy disk. Police computer experts linked it to a computer at Christ Lutheran Church used to print an agenda by Dennis Rader, the church council president. Police secretly took DNA from Rader's daughter Kerri and matched it to a sample found in Josie's body thirty-one years earlier. That was all the evidence needed to convince them that Rader and BTK were one and the same.

When Wichita police announced his arrest, there was universal shock that such an 'ordinary' man could have performed such extraordinarily evil crimes. Former FBI profiler Gregg McCrary, who studied the Rader case, said: 'BTK had committed such monstrous crimes that we wanted the guy to be a monster, drooling and with one eye in the middle of his forehead. But we look right through them because they fit in society well.'

Robert Beattie, author of a book on the BTK case, said: 'His external life was a mask of sanity. His internal life was one of violent fantasies. He will go down in the annals of crime as an evil Walter Mitty.'

At his trial in August 2005, the gruesome details of Rader's crimes transfixed the court hearing and revealed him as the embodiment of evil.

The bespectacled 60-year-old looked relaxed as he listened to the horrendous details of his crimes. He spoke calmly as he confirmed the admissions he had made to police. And he chillingly admitted planning a further murder, saying: 'There was one picked out. I was thinking about it but I was beginning to slow down.'

Telling how he bound, tortured and strangled the Otero family in 1974, Rader said: 'I strangled dogs and cats but I never strangled a person before . . . so I really didn't know how much pressure you had to put on a person or how long it would take. When Mrs Otero woke back up, she was pretty upset with what's going on and at that point in time, I strangled her.'

He had then taken poor Josie to the basement, stripped her and asked if her daddy had a camera for a picture. When she said no, he strung her up from a sewer pipe, masturbating as he watched the life drain from her.

In a written confession, he said: 'Josephine, when I hung her really turn(ed) me on. Her pleading for mercy . . . then the rope took (hold); she helpless; staring at me with wide terror fill(ed) eyes, the rope getting tighter-tighter.'

Rader admitted ten murders and was jailed for a minimum of 175 years, with no chance of parole. It was the longest sentence the judge could deliver, as the crimes were committed before Kansas reintroduced capital punishment.

Alexander Pichushkin

'Chessboard Killer' disposed of his victims in a city's sewers

The huge network of powerful sewer systems beneath Bitsevsky Park serves all of southern Moscow. It is where many of the dozens of victims of one of Russia's most notorious serial killers ended up. It was not a dignified end for any of them, of course, but when they were hurled alive into one of the sewer's access pits, their plight was even more revolting. They would swim around in the filth, scrabbling for a hand-hold on the slimy sides, until finally being sucked into the foul labyrinth.

The vast, wooded park was the preferred killing field of Alexander Pichushkin, who lured his victims there with the promise of a bottle of beer or a shot of vodka. Occasionally, he would suggest a game of chess. And after disposing of each victim, he would return to his nearby apartment and place a coin or vodka bottle stopper on one more square of a chessboard.

That is the way the 'Chessboard Killer', as Pichushkin came to be known, recorded his grisly crimes, attaching a number to another square of the board every time he struck. By the time he was caught, Pichushkin had filled in sixty-two of the sixty-four squares.

Since his birth on 9 April 1974, Alexander Yuryevich Pichushkin had lived with his mother, Natalya, in a typical Soviet-era, high-rise block in the south Moscow suburbs, not far from Bitsevsky Park. He never knew his father, who walked out on the family.

Natalya Pichushkin charted the beginning of her son's downfall to when he suffered a blow to the head after an accident on a swing at the age of 4. He subsequently spent time in an institute for children with special needs and his spelling was badly affected. His mother said he might also have been affected by the sudden death of his grandfather, with whom he also lived. There were suggestions that he was briefly treated in the psychiatric section of a local hospital.

Pichushkin's neighbour as a boy, Svetlana Mortyakova, remembers the future serial killer as 'a pleasant kid', always polite and someone 'who loved animals'. She once found him in tears in the stairwell of the block of flats they shared, speechless with grief over the death of his cat.

Whereas most Russians were conscripted into the army at 18, Pichushkin failed the medical. Despite training as a carpenter, he never worked as one. A drink problem meant that the only jobs he could hold down were menial ones, such as supermarket shelf-stacking. Yet neighbours insist Pichushkin never became violent. 'Vodka affects people in different ways,' recalled one, 'but he just became weak and used to collapse at my feet.'

As a young man, Pichushkin had neither friends nor money and girls didn't like him. He lived an ordinary, boring, everyday life – yet he strove to be different. After his grandfather died, he spent much of his time wandering around Bitsevsky Park, stopping to smoke and drink beer or vodka on the benches under the trees. He was well known to the drunks and itinerants who passed their time there. Until his arrest in the summer of 2006, the 32-year-old spent his working days in a supermarket, his evenings in the park, and his nights at the apartment with his ageing mother.

Pichushkin had first killed fourteen years earlier, in 1992, when he was just 18 years old, murdering the boyfriend of a neighbour he had fallen in love with. He later killed the girl herself, whose body was found in Bitsevsky Park. Subsequent murders were sporadic but in 2005 the supermarket shelf-stacker embarked on a slaying spree. At one stage, police were uncovering one body every week – most having the serial killer's hallmark of a smashed skull, with the neck of a vodka bottle thrust into the gaping wound.

Most of his victims were homeless drifters or drunks. Others were elderly or homeless men who would not have been able to put up much of a defence and whose disappearances went largely unnoticed, which is how Pichushkin managed to evade capture for many years.

Pichushkin would lure his targets to join him in the park with the promise of a drinking session. Occasionally, he would suggest a game of chess or invite them to see the grave of his beloved pet dog. Once in the park's wooded areas, his victims were either strangled or killed with a blow to the skull from a hammer or blunt object. He would always attack from behind in order to stop blood from soaking his clothes, and finally he would stick the neck of a vodka bottle into his victim's skull, ensuring that they did not survive. He could be particularly cruel. The body of one woman was found with tiny stakes hammered into her skull and around her eyes.

Seventeen of his prey were left casually on the ground. But most of the bodies were disposed of by dumping them in one of the access pits to the sewers that ran beneath the park – including that of his youngest victim, a homeless boy known only as Mitka who was just 9 years old.

This meant that those who were not killed instantly ended their agonies by drowning in the subterranean filth. As many as forty people were believed to have been disposed of in this way while still breathing. According to Moscow police investigator Valeria Suchova: 'Those people who were thrown down into the sewers were, if I can say so, rather lucky, because their deaths were pretty instant. There are such massive water flows and such a huge water pressure that when we tried to put a mannequin inside the sewer to see what it was like down there, it was simply torn apart.'

One of his victims who survived this ordeal, Maria Viricheva, a shop clerk from Tatarstan, told how Pichushkin lured her into a secluded part of the forest on the premise of showing her some black market goods. Viricheva had met Pichushkin in February 2002 near Kakhovskaya metro station. At the time, she was pregnant, had just split up from her boyfriend and was desperate to make ends meet. She was crying when he approached her and offered to sell her some cameras, which he told her he'd hidden in the park.

Pichushkin took her to a remote corner of the park and told her the cameras were in the sewer. He then grabbed her by her hair and pushed her down the 8-metre deep pit. She said she 'feverishly fumbled about in the walls of the tube and swam around in the mulch for a whole hour' before she could grip the side.

Despite Viricheva's detailed statement about who her attempted killer was and where he could be found, the local policeman taking her statement asked her to drop her complaint because he didn't want to deal with what he thought was needless work on an unimportant case. The investigation was never pursued and an opportunity was missed to catch the killer much earlier and possibly save more than twenty lives. When Pichushkin was finally arrested four years later, and the connection made with Viricheva's case, the officer who had first interviewed her went on the run and a warrant had to be issued for his arrest.

By the time of Pichushkin's capture in 2006, Moscow was in the grip of terror as the death toll mounted. Suspects were regularly picked up, interrogated and released. Initial suspicion fell on the inmates of a psychiatric unit close to Bitsevsky Park. In February 2006, police shot a man in the leg after learning that somebody resembling the suspect had been spotted in the park. He was later released. So too was a transvestite with a hammer in his purse. It transpired that he was carrying it for protection against the mysterious mass murderer.

Police finally caught the real killer in June 2006 after discovering that his final victim, his supermarket colleague Marina Moskalyova, 36, had left a note for her son saying she was going for a walk in the woods with Pichushkin. He denied involvement until detectives produced video surveillance footage of the couple strolling together just before the murder.

When he finally confessed, Pichushkin admitted that he even knew of the note his victim had left for her son. But he said flippantly: 'While we were walking in the park, while we were talking, I just kept thinking, "Kill her or forget it?" In the end, I decided to risk it. I was, after all, already in the mood.'

Under arrest, the 32-year-old killer confessed: 'I liked to watch their agony. For me, a life without murder is like a life without food for anyone else. I felt like the father of all these people, since it was I who opened the door for them to another world.'

He also admitted that killing gave him orgasms. 'Your first murder is like your first love,' he said, 'you never forget it. And the closer the person is to you, the more pleasant it is to kill him. It's more emotional.'

A team of doctors at Russia's leading psychiatric institute spent over six months analysing Pichushkin's background and psychiatric history. One of them, Dr Yevgeniy Makushkin, issued an official statement of the seemingly obvious: 'Pichushkin wasn't happy in his private life; he just did his job and led a lonely existence. The pattern of behaviour that we were witnessing was very complicated, but there was indeed a certain pattern: a striving to murder, and to aggressive-sadistic activity.'

Another psychologist, Mikhail Vinogradov, interpreted the murders as being prompted by anger at Pichushkin's grandfather for abandoning him. There was also a 'sexual subtext', he said, the killer having described his criminal career as 'a perpetual orgasm'.

Psychoanalyst Tatyana Drusinova reported that his love of chess, which ironically he couldn't play, was a clue to his character. She said: 'Alexander Pichushkin is detached from human beings, who are no more than wooden dolls – like chess pieces to him.'

One of the mysteries puzzling prosecutors was that the motivations for the slayings were so flimsy. Pichushkin told police he knew 'maybe twenty' of his victims and, under interrogation in 2006, attempted to explain one particular killing – of his neighbour, Valery Kulyazhov, because of a row over their dogs. Pichushkin's beloved mongrel had apparently sniffed the pet of Mr Kulyazhov, who shouted: 'Take away that enormous mongrel mutt.' Pichushkin did not forget the insult – but waited all of ten years before killing Mr Kulyazhov.

In interviews before his trial, Pichushkin stated that he saw himself as 'a god of the wood'. Before he killed, he would listen to his victims' life stories, lecture them about how they should live and then kill them. In his eyes, they were sinners. A journalist who followed the case observed: 'Since he was arrested, he has always seemed calm and full of self-respect. He even refused to carry on with the trial before all his victims' families were assembled so that he could look into the eyes of every single one of them. He wants glory.'

However, experts at Moscow's Serbsky Institute, Russia's main psychiatric clinic, declared that Pichushkin was not mentally ill. As his actions 'were purposeful and he was fully aware of the consequences', he was judged sane and fit to stand trial.

Thus, under the gaze of the world's media, the 'Chessboard Killer' had one last game to play. On 13 September 2007, Russia's most prolific murderer went on trial in Moscow accused of causing the deaths of forty-nine people. It was the culmination of a killing spree that had lasted for over fifteen years and had kept an entire city in fear.

In a moment of high drama, Moscow prosecutor Yury Syomin claimed that the accused 'dreamed of going down in history by surpassing Andrei Chikatilo' – the so-called 'Rostov Ripper' who, before the Pichushkin case came to light, was Russia's previously most notorious serial killer. Chikatilo, a paedophile who mutilated and ate some of his victims' remains during a twelve-year killing spree, was executed in 1994 for the murder of fifty-two women and children in the southern city of Rostov. Pichushkin had at first attempted to confess to sixty-two slayings – although prosecutors found sufficient evidence for only forty-eight charges of murder.

It was suggested that Pichushkin's bid to surpass Andrei Chikatilo's body count could explain why he had changed his modus operandi from disposing of his victims in the sewers, where they simply disappeared, to leaving them in the open, where they were almost guaranteed to be found. That action would seem to imply that he wanted full credit for what he was doing.

Pichushkin had originally told police that he had planned to carry out sixty-four killings, one for each square on a chess-board. But he later denied this, saying he would have carried on killing indefinitely if he had not been arrested. 'I never would have stopped, never,' he said. 'They saved a lot of lives by catching me.'

One of the detectives who had headed the murder investigation watched Pichushkin in the courtroom and commented: 'It was a real performance for him. He wanted the attention and that was the place where he could it. There was the jury, there was the press, there were the prosecutors and judge, and it was all about him, and he was really pleased about that. He spoke with great pleasure in court about all the things he did. He was really enjoying it.'

It was Alexander Pichushkin's moment in the limelight and he played it to the full. He was asked if he had any regrets. Pichushkin paused for a minute, and, without an iota of remorse, answered: 'Yes, I do regret one thing. I regret that you arrested me so early. I was planning to murder another woman in two days' time.'

Pichushkin was convicted of forty-eight murders and three counts of attempted murder. With the death penalty no longer in force, he was jailed for life, with the first fifteen years in solitary confinement.

CHAPTER 17

Gerald Gallego & Charlene Williams

Couple who kidnapped 'slaves' and buried victim alive

Gerald Armond Gallego was born in 1946 into an environment almost guaranteed to produce the killer he was to become. He never met his father, Gerald Albert Gallego, as he was in San Quentin jail for burglary at the time of his birth. After being paroled, his father moved to Mississippi where he continued his criminal activities, culminating in his execution in Mississippi's gas chamber in 1955 for the murder of two police officers. Gerald's mother was a known prostitute in Sacramento, and young Gerald served as a runner for various pimps during the early 1950s.

By contrast, Charlene Williams was born in 1956 into a middle-class family; her father was an executive with a national grocery chain. She was an only child with an extremely high IQ and a gift for playing the violin. However, she dabbled in drugs and alcohol while still at high school and dropped out of college. Two unsuccessful marriages swiftly followed.

By the time he met Charlene in 1977, Gerald Gallego Jr had a police record that started with a burglary when he was 6 years old. A sexual offender at 12, he was jailed for armed robbery at the age of 22. He went on the run in 1978 after his daughter complained to police that he had been abusing her from the age of 6.

Gallego had first married when he was 17 and by the time he started going out with Charlene, when she was 21 and he was 32, he had been married and divorced five times. He charmed Charlene with a dozen roses following their first date, and within just a few weeks the two had moved in together. Gallego dominated Williams from the outset, but the young Charlene found him exciting, thrilling at his fantasy of capturing and using young women as sex slaves.

Gallego gave his girlfriend her first assignment in September 1978, ordering her to seek out two suitable 'slaves' at a shopping centre in Sacramento. She lured 17-year-old Rhonda Scheffler and 16-year-old Kippi Vaught into the back of Gallego's white van with the promise of smoking some pot. Once inside, Gallego bound them with tape, raped and beat them, before shooting them and leaving their bodies in a ditch.

From then onwards, their modus operandi was set. The pair would tour central California, southern Oregon and Nevada by van, procuring victims to fulfil Gallego's sex-slave fantasies. The girls would be lured into the van with the promise of drugs, whence Gallego would pounce on them, rape them and murder them while Charlene sat coolly in the front seat.

The couple's second pair of victims were 14-year-old Brenda Judd and 13-year-old Sandra Colley, abducted on their way home from Washoe County Fair. Charlene again lured the unsuspecting young girls into the back of the van and watched in the rear view mirror as Gallego repeatedly raped them. He then became the spectator as Charlene forced the girls to perform sexual acts with each other, before Gerald bludgeoned them to death with a shovel. They were thought to have run away to join the carnival and their murder was only discovered when Charlene confessed to it at her trial in 1982.

In April 1980, they used the shopping mall as a hunting ground again and picked up two 17-year-olds, Stacey Redican and Karen Twiggs. Williams offered them free drugs and a ride home but instead they were repeatedly raped by the pair before Gallego killed them both, this time with a hammer, and disposed of their bodies.

Two months later, Gerald picked up 21-year-old Linda Aguilar, who was four months' pregnant, and offered her a lift at Gold Beach, Oregon. Charlene drove while Gerald raped Linda in the back. Her bound body was found in a shallow grave with her skull shattered. However, a post mortem revealed that she and her unborn baby had been buried alive.

The killers had been living under the alias of Mr and Mrs Stephen Feil for some time, but on 1 June 1980, they married for the second time using these names, possibly because Williams discovered she was pregnant. Her baby was born in custody in January 1981 and was raised by her mother Mercedes Williams.

Shortly after Gallego's 34th birthday in July 1980, the couple were enjoying an evening out together in a bar. Despite paying the barmaid little attention throughout the evening, Gerald insisted on waiting for her in the car park at the end of her shift. He forced Virginia Mochel into his van at gunpoint and took her back to their apartment, where he subjected her to repeated violent rape, after which he strangled her. Throughout the attack, Charlene was calmly watching the television in the living room. They then drove the van out into the countryside and dumped Virginia's body in the undergrowth.

Watching couples leaving a dance in the early hours of 2 November 1980, Gallego was attracted to 22-year-old Craig Miller and his fiancée, 21-year-old Mary Elizabeth Sowers. He ordered the young couple into the back of the van at gunpoint, but was seen in the act by friends of the couple who took down the registration number.

Charlene drove them out into the countryside once again and Gerald quickly despatched Craig, firing three shots directly into his head. They took the terrified Mary back to their apartment, where Gallego raped her for hours on end. When he was finally satisfied, Charlene again drove into the country, to a different location this time, and Mary was murdered, shot at point-blank range in the head.

Because of the sharp-eyed witness who had noted the number of their van, the couple's trail of murders was now at an end. The police closed in on them and, with the help of Williams's parents, who informed the police when she contacted them asking for money, FBI agents finally apprehended them in Omaha, Nebraska.

The 24-year-old Charlene plea-bargained to testify against her husband in exchange for giving details about the murders, thus avoiding the death penalty. She claimed Gallego was violent and abusive towards her and that she had been forced to comply with his sick fantasies. She provided details of the ten murders and informed the police of the whereabouts of the bodies of young Brenda Judd and Sandra Colley. She was sentenced to sixteen years in jail and was set free in 1997.

Gerald Gallego was sentenced to death in both California in June 1983 and again in Nevada a year later. He remained on Death Row through a series of appeals, but died in July 2002 of rectal cancer, which had spread to his liver and lungs.

CHAPTER 18

Gary Heidnik

Kidnap killer collected a harem he kept chained in basement

The son of an alcoholic mother and brutal father, Gary Heidnik was never destined to make anything of his life. But no-one could ever have envisaged that the man with a high IQ would turn his mind to murder in the most terrifying and depraved way. In under a year, Heidnik kidnapped a series of women and subjected them to unspeakable horror in his desire to fulfil his fantasy of having a harem of sex slaves.

Heidnik was born in the Cleveland suburb of Eastlake, Ohio, on 22 November 1943, to Michael and Ellen Heidnik. A second son, Terry, was born a year later. When Heidnik was 2 years old, his father divorced his mother because of her alcoholism but she looked after the two little boys for four years before handing them over to her former husband and his new wife. Ellen Heidnik later committed suicide. An already disturbed childhood was made worse by Michael Heidnik's treatment of the boys. When Gary Heidnik wet the bed, his father would humiliate him by hanging the soiled sheets from his bedroom window in full view of the neighbours. As well as suffering mental and physical abuse at home, Heidnik had to tolerate bullying at school. He was an easy target – a strange-looking boy with a misshapen head (said to be the result of falling out of a tree) – and an unusually high IQ of 130.

At 14, Heidnik enrolled at Staunton Military Academy with the aim of pursuing his ambition to join the army. He then attended a high school before dropping out and joining the US Army when he was 17. It was a short-lived military career. Although described as 'excellent' during his basic training, Heidnik was already starting to show mental problems. He was turned down for several positions in the army, including the military police, finally being accepted to train as a medic in San Antonio, Texas, before being transferred to the 46th Army Surgical Hospital in Landstuhl, West Germany.

It was in August 1962 that Heidnik's true mental state was discovered. He had been admitted to hospital complaining of a number of symptoms including headaches, dizziness and blurred vision. It was also noticed that he displayed psychological problems, and a couple of months later, he was diagnosed with a schizoid personality disorder and discharged from the army with a full pension.

This did not stop Heidnik continuing to work in the medical profession. He qualified as a nurse and for a short time ironically worked as a psychiatric nurse at a veterans' hospital before being fired for poor attendance and rudeness to patients. Heidnik himself was receiving treatment for his mental illness, first being prescribed a strong tranquilliser and then spending the following years in and out of psychiatric hospitals at least twenty-one times. In between treatments, he attempted suicide – thirteen times in all, including overdoses, hanging, crashing his car and eating a broken light bulb. In 1971, he sought a new way out of his mental turmoil, founding his own church, the United Church of the Ministers of God. It originally had only five members, but by 1986 the church was thriving.

But while all this was going on, Heidnik was also killing women. It had become his 'hobby', for having invested his pension cleverly, he was now worth almost a million dollars.

Heidnik sought out black women with low intelligence as his sexual partners. One of them, Anjeanette Davidson, gave birth to a daughter Maxine in 1978. That same year, she and Heidnik visited her sister, Alberta, in a mental institution in Harrisburg, Pennsylvania. The two were given permission to take the young woman out for the day. Alberta never returned. She was later found in the basement of Heidnik's house. Alberta, with the mental age of a toddler, had been raped and sodomised. Heidnik was arrested and charged with kidnapping, rape, unlawful restraint, false imprisonment, involuntary deviant sexual intercourse and interfering with the custody of a committed person. He was found guilty and sentenced to three to seven years in prison, although he served only four years for the crime, following an appeal.

Heidnik's mental state worsened and one day while in prison he handed a note to a guard saying that he could no longer speak as the devil had 'shoved a cookie down his throat'. Heidnik did not speak for the next two and a half years. He was released in April 1983 under the supervision of a mental health programme. His daughter Maxine, meanwhile, was taken away from her mother and placed with foster parents.

After his release, Heidnik signed up with a marriage agency and began a correspondence with a 'mail order bride', Betty Disto, who eventually travelled to America from the Philippines and married him on 3 October 1985. She left him three months later after he forced his sick sexual predilections on her, including forcing her to watch him having sex with prostitutes. One day she found her husband in bed with three women.

With the help of the local Filipino community, Betty managed to escape the clutches of her husband. It was only after she left that she discovered she was pregnant with Heidnik's child, a son she named Jesse John Disto. She requested child support payments from Heidnik, who, discovering he had another child, formed a sick plan . . . He would create a baby-making factory in his basement and kidnap and impregnate ten women with his children.

His first victim was 25-year-old prostitute Josefina Rivera, whom he kidnapped on Thanksgiving Day in 1986. Josefina had left her apartment in a slum area of Philadelphia after an argument with her boyfriend. She was stopped by Heidnik as he cruised around in his silver and white Cadillac Coupe de Ville. Arriving at Heidnik's home, 3520 North Marshall Street, the woman noticed a Rolls Royce parked outside. She was further taken aback to see the kitchen decorated with coins and the hallway covered with one and five dollar bills.

After the two had had sex, Heidnik forced Josefina into his basement. He dragged her onto a dirty mattress, attached metal clamps to her ankles and connected them to the end of a chain. He then applied glue to the clamps and dried them with a hair-drier. He fastened the other end around a large pipe. When he had finished, Heidnik told Josefina to sit up, laid his head in her lap and went to sleep. Later Heidnik told his prisoner that all he had ever wanted was a large family. Then he raped her. When she cried out for help, he beat her and turned up a radio to drown her screams.

Two days later, Josefina was joined by another woman, 24-year-old Sandra Lindsay. This victim was retarded and described Heidnik as a good friend with whom she regularly had sex. Heidnik had kidnapped her after he found out she had aborted his baby. He later forced her to write a note home saying she had run away, but Sandra's mother became suspicious and alerted police to her daughter's relationship with a man she knew only as Gary. She even gave the police Heidnik's address and telephone number. But a police officer assigned to the case failed to pursue the investigation further after failing to get an answer on the phone and after calling at the house.

That Christmas, Heidnik cruised the streets looking for another woman. He found 19-year-old Lisa Thomas, who was on her way to visit a girlfriend's house. Believing her to be a prostitute, Heidnik made a suggestive comment. An angry Lisa refuted this but accepted Heidnik's apology and took up his offer of a lift. He took her to his house, drugged and raped her before making her join his other slaves.

Heidnik's next victim was Deborah Dudley, 23. Upon her arrival, Heidnik began forcing the women to have sex with each other while he watched. In January, a fifth woman, 18-year-old Jacqueline Askins, was brought to Heidnik's home. The women were all subjected to beatings, torture and rape – dressed only in shirts so that Heidnik could force himself upon them more easily.

Feeling totally in control and wielding such power over his victims, Heidnik became even more demented. He used shock therapy on his prisoners and shoved screwdrivers into their ears when he became paranoid that they were plotting against him. Only Josefina, who pretended to be an ally of Heidnik, was spared this agonising way of deafening his prisoners.

Sandra Lindsay succumbed to the excessive torture and died in February after hanging by her wrists for a week. Heidnik carried her body upstairs, dismembered it with a power saw and then cooked up her flesh, putting her ribs in an oven and boiling her head on a stove. He then mixed the parts with dog food and force-fed the resulting mush to his other victims.

By now, Heidnik had dug a pit within the basement, used for what he called 'isolation punishment'. In it he would place his prisoners before covering it with plywood and heavy weights. It would then be filled with water and an electric current applied. On 18 March 1987, Deborah Dudley, who had angered Heidnik by her defiance, was placed in the pit and electrocuted. Josefina Rivera helped Heidnik dump the body in a New Jersey park after he had forced her to write a 'confession' to the woman's murder in case she ever betrayed him. Josefina was thereafter allowed to become Heidnik's 'companion', accompanying him on outings to restaurants and on shopping expeditions.

Another prisoner, 24-year-old prostitute Agnes Adams, was brought in as a replacement for Deborah. Her ordeal was not to last as long as the others. On 24 March, Josefina managed to escape after Heidnik loosened her bonds and trusted her to walk around freely. She ran to the house of her boyfriend, Vincent Nelson, who was horrified at the state she was in after four months with Heidnik. The police were called, and at first found it hard to believe Josefina's story. But when she led them to Heidnik's house, they found the surviving women huddled in the basement – and some of Sandra's body parts in his freezer and fridge. Deborah Dudley's body was also later discovered.

Ludicrously, Heidnik claimed the women had already been in the house when he moved in. Charged with numerous crimes, including the two murders, Heidnik came to trial on 20 June 1988. He was convicted on all eighteen counts on 6 July. This was despite attempts by his defence counsel, Charles Peruto Jr, to persuade the jury that Heidnik was legally insane. It was a claim successfully disproved by the prosecution, which referred to the killer's well-organised financial dealings. Heidnik's financial advisor, Robert Kirkpatrick from Merrill Lynch, described Heidnik as 'an astute investor who knew exactly what he was doing'.

Heidnik was incarcerated at the State Correctional Institute of Pittsburgh, where he attempted to kill himself with an over-dose of a prescribed drug, thorazine, in January 1999. Other suicide attempts followed before he was executed by lethal injection at Rockview prison, Pennsylvania, on 6 July 1999. Upon being informed that his son was about to be put to death, Heidnik's father said he 'simply wasn't interested ...'

CHAPTER 19

Gary Taylor

Blunders that freed 'woman hater' to become a serial slayer

Gary Addison Taylor was born in Michigan in 1936 and spent his early years in Florida, enjoying a seemingly normal childhood. But by the time he reached his teenage years, the humiliation he felt his mother had subjected him to when younger led to him focussing on women as hate figures who had to be 'punished'. At the age of 18, Taylor started to hang out at bus stations waiting for his prey – lone women. As they alighted from a bus, he would follow them and strike from behind with a wrench or hammer. He was eventually charged with attacking a woman with a wrench as she stepped off a bus in St Petersburg, Florida. Incredibly, a jury acquitted him – just one of a series of blunders which would result in Taylor later confessing to four murders but being suspected of as many as twenty.

Taylor continued his stalking and violent attacks on women and was sentenced to a term of imprisonment at a juvenile centre. When he was released, aged 21, he returned to Michigan. Now his hatred of women took a new and more dramatic turn. The itinerant machinist drove through four Detroit suburbs firing at women. He always operated at night as women walked through the streets alone. He wounded two, but miraculously none of his victims were killed.

Taylor's manic shootings saw him labelled 'The Phantom Sniper' and 'The Royal Oak Sniper' in the local press. When finally arrested, he was described in court by a psychiatrist as 'unreasonably hostile to women and this makes it very possible that he might very well kill a person'. Taylor was declared insane and committed to Michigan's Ionia State Hospital; three years later he was transferred to the Lafayette Clinic in Detroit. In all, Taylor received psychiatric treatment at various hospitals on and off for eleven years. But in between, he continued his violent hate campaign against women.

Once, out on a pass from hospital to attend a welding class, Taylor talked his way into a Detroit woman's home, then raped and robbed her. By the next year, out on another pass, he threatened a rooming-house manager and her daughter with an 18-inch butcher's knife. He was not put on trial in either incident; instead he was sent back to Ionia State Hospital.

In 1972, the authorities blundered again and Taylor was released from the Michigan Center for Forensic Psychiatry in Ypsilanti. Despite his continuing violence and his confession of feeling a 'compulsion to hurt women' – as well as being declared medically 'insane' – Taylor was considered safe enough to be released from his permanent residency at mental institutions and to become an out-patient. Under Michigan law, a person acquitted of a crime by reason of insanity cannot be kept indefinitely in a mental institution; he must be periodically certified mentally ill and dangerous to himself or the community. The psychiatric centre's director, Dr Ames Robey, diagnosed Taylor's condition as a character disorder and not a treatable mental illness. Robey did not think Taylor was dangerous as long as he took medication, regularly turned up for hospital appointments and did not drink.

This was not a regime that suited Gary Taylor, however. Towards the end of 1973, he stopped turning up for his hospital appointments. The authorities made the fatal mistake of not reporting Taylor's disappearance to the National Crime Information Centre in Washington, DC, for fourteen months. By then, despite his obsessive hatred towards women, Taylor had met and married a secretary called Helen and moved first to Onsted, Michigan, and later to the suburbs of Seattle, Washington. Taylor and his wife would later separate and he settled down in Houston. But by then he had also murdered at least four women with a machete in three different states.

What makes Taylor stand out in serial killer history is the change in his method of attack. Normally, such a killer has a 'trademark' pattern from which he does not deviate. But during his chilling criminal spree, Taylor changed from hammer attacks to gun attacks. He also became a calculating and clever 'conman killer'. Now he would telephone a victim and claim there was an emergency, such as a fire, in her place of work or apartment – and then attack the woman as she drove up and got out of her car. He posed as an FBI agent at the door of another of his victims.

Two women murdered by Taylor were from Ohio: 25-year-old Lee Fletcher and 23-year-old Deborah Heneman. They were buried in Taylor's back yard before he fled from his home in Onsted, Michigan, and moved west to Seattle. There, one November night, he abducted and killed young housewife Vonnie Stuth. Police officers traced him to Enumclaw, Washington, where he initially co-operated, allowing himself to be interrogated but refusing to take a polygraph (lie detector) test. However, because there was no record of Taylor on the NCIC listings, officers involved in the murder inquiry did not know his background or that he was officially a fugitive. So they let him go. By the time Michigan authorities finally entered Taylor's name and details into the national computer, he had vanished again, this time heading for Texas.

Taylor continued his attacks, but randomly decided whether he should kill his victim or rape her and let her live. On 20 May 1975, he was picked up in Houston, Texas, on a charge of sexual assault and confessed to four murders. Two days later, police in Michigan found the bodies of the two murdered Toledo girls, Lee Fletcher and Deborah Heneman, wrapped in plastic bags, buried outside the bedroom window of Taylor's former Onsted home. And in Enumclaw, Washington, police found the body of 19-year-old Vonnie Stuth behind another house where Taylor had lived. Vonnie had been killed on 28 November 1974. Her husband Todd had tried to report her missing as soon as she disappeared, only to be waved away by a desk policeman who said that a person had to be missing for forty-eight hours before action could be taken. It was, of course, yet another fatal error in the whole sorry saga of Gary Taylor's slayings.

Taylor signed confessions to Vonnie's murder as well as that of Houston victim Susan Jackson, 21. Further police investigations cleared Taylor of six other Washington murders, now blamed on another notorious killer, Ted Bundy. But investigators in Texas, Michigan, and California suspect Taylor in as many as twenty unsolved homicides. When news of his arrest in

Houston reached Taylor's estranged wife in San Diego, she said Taylor had once told her that he had killed four people in Onsted. Taylor admitted to four murders, but later insisted to a Houston Justice of the Peace that police had beaten the confessions out of him, a claim that was later dismissed. Taylor was also charged with three counts of aggravated sexual abuse, one of attempted aggravated rape, and the rape of a 16-year-old pregnant girl.

Convicted on the four counts to which he had confessed, Taylor was sentenced to life imprisonment. As observers noted, Taylor would not have been able to become a full-blown killer if he had been incarcerated in Michigan all those years ago. But a ruling by the State Supreme Court upheld the law that the cases of the mentally ill, including criminals, should be reviewed every six months. The problem comes in defining mental illness. In several recent Michigan homicide cases, psychiatrists have disagreed on whether those who committed the crimes should be confined. Gary Taylor was such a case. And so he was set free to kill and kill again.

CHAPTER 20

Ian Brady & Myra Hindley

'Moors Murders': crimes against children sickened a nation

Standing fully 35 feet high and dating back over forty years, previously unseen official files were released in 2008 relating to the most reviled woman in British criminal history: Myra Hindley. They provided a fresh insight into the mind of this peroxide-blonde monster. In the same year, fresh revelations about her sinister partner, Ian Brady, came to light, raising the spectre that he and his partner had killed many more victims than previously suspected. The banner headlines that these two stories caused were extraordinary, given the length of time since the crimes they had committed. That is because Brady and Hindley – the so-called 'Moors Murderers' – hold a unique position in the annals of infamy.

To an entire British generation who lived in the more innocent age of half a century ago, the names of Brady and Hindley became synonymous with pure evil. Even today, in a world hardened by violent crime, their vile deeds set them apart as monsters of a very special breed. The pair have become objects of hatred like no other English serial killers. It was Hindley, because she was a woman and because her crimes were against children, who aroused the greatest revulsion. But it was Brady who was the driving force, the Svengali who turned a normal young woman into a willing participant in perversions, torture and child-killing.

Brady was a sadistic fetishist who drew a willing Hindley into his wild games. They took pictures of themselves having sex while dressed in leather, brandishing whips and acting out Nazi crimes. And all too soon, the games turned into reality.

Between 1962 and 1965, Brady and Hindley abducted, tortured and murdered at least five, possibly eight, children or teenagers. Most of the bodies were buried on bleak Saddleworth Moor, on the hills outside the city of Manchester where they lived.

Some dark destiny had brought these two together. Brady, born in 1938, was the illegitimate son of a Glasgow waitress. A sullen, moody boy, his first court appearance was for burglary in 1951 when he was 13. He was put on probation twice. In 1954 he moved to Manchester to live with his mother and her new husband. He took a job in a brewery but was caught stealing lead and served a year in Borstal. After his release, it seemed he had finished with his criminal ways and he settled into a job as a clerk. That is when he first met Hindley.

The monsters' paths first crossed in 1961 when Hindley was just 19 years old. She was employed as a typist at the same company, a chemical supply firm. Hindley meticulously kept a diary after making Brady's acquaintance. One entry read: 'Ian wore a black shirt and looked smashing. I love him.' Their affair began a year later.

Myra Hindley had walked into Brady's life at a time when his mind was growing more and more twisted and his obsession with sadism had become all-consuming. The instant hold he had over Hindley has never been fully understood. But right from the start, she eagerly participated in his fetishes. They both wore leather and acted out Nazi crimes together. They took pictures of themselves having sex and with whips. But this was not enough for the evil couple. Brady wanted to inflict his perversions on the innocent – and Hindley was more than a willing partner. In the months that followed, she showed herself to be a woman without mercy, someone who would assist her sadistic lover as he toyed with his victims before participating in their tortured final demise.

Their first known victim was 16-year-old Pauline Reade, from the Gorton area of Manchester, who disappeared in July 1963. As with all their victims, Hindley was the one who lured her into Brady's clutches. Pauline was told by her neighbour Hindley that she had lost a glove on Saddleworth Moor and wanted the girl to help her search for it. Brady, who was following them, hit Pauline over the head with a shovel and raped the girl before cutting her throat.

Four months later, Brady told Hindley 'It is time to do another one,' and 12-year-old John Kilbride went missing. The boy was said to have gone with the couple 'like a lamb to the slaughter'. Once on the moor, he was held down and molested by Brady before being strangled and buried in the boggy soil.

Another 12-year-old, Keith Bennett, vanished in June 1964. It later emerged that Hindley had asked him to carry some boxes of shopping for her before Brady used the lost glove story to lure him onto the moor. There the boy was abused and strangled, Brady taking photographs of the body before burying it.

Ten-year-old Lesley Ann Downey disappeared while attending a Christmas fair on 26 December. She was taken to Brady's home and forced to pose nude for pornographic photographs before being sexually tortured and strangled.

Ten months elapsed before Brady and Hindley struck again. In October 1965, Brady met 17-year-old Edward Evans, believed to be a homosexual. There was a special reason why Brady wanted to entice this victim to his home, where he had also invited Hindley's brother-in-law David Smith. Brady talked to Smith about previous murders but then became fearful that he would go to the police. It was therefore vital that Smith was present at the murder of Evans, so that he too would be implicated. In front of the horrified Smith, Brady then launched his fatal, bloody attack on Evans with a hatchet – Brady ensuring that Smith's fingerprints were also on the weapon.

After the murder, Brady boasted to Smith: 'It's the messiest yet. It normally only takes one blow.' Edward's body was wrapped in plastic and taken upstairs. Smith later recalled that the couple then sat around laughing and drinking wine, Hindley still wearing her blood-soaked shoes.

The attempt to involve Smith was a fatal mistake. What he had witnessed so disturbed him that he went to the police. Arrested, Brady tried to put the blame onto Smith and to keep Hindley in the clear. Under questioning, Brady made mistakes and the police were able to trip him up on several of his denials. Hindley, however, was a tougher nut to crack and never wavered under interrogation. She simply stated: 'I didn't do it. Ian didn't do it. I am saying nothing.' Hindley was not arrested for four days following the murder of Evans, and in that time she managed to destroy some evidence. But the case against them was already solid.

A search of Brady's house revealed a book with John Kilbride's name in it. A ticket led police to a luggage locker at Manchester Central railway station. The two suitcases found there contained sex and torture books, whips, coshes and other items used for perverted activities – plus nine pornographic pictures of Lesley Ann Downey. Another photograph showed Hindley posing next to John Kilbride's shallow grave on Saddleworth Moor. This enabled police to locate the boy's grave and the grave of Lesley Ann Downey.

However, the most horrifying discovery was the recording made of the dying cries of poor Lesley Ann. Tough cops wept when they first listened to the tape. A senior detective screamed 'Turn it off, turn it off' as he covered his ears from the sound of the child's pleading and sobbing. And when the tape was finally played in a hushed courtroom, hardened reporters were also reduced to tears.

The trial of Hindley and Brady began on 19 April 1966, at Chester Assizes. According to Hindley's confession, Brady told her that he had strangled John Kilbride with a thin piece of string and had cut Pauline Reade's throat. But it was the production of the cassette tape that was the most damning evidence. No one who sat in court that day would ever forget the harrowing recording played to them. It was of Lesley Ann's voice, begging for her mother and pleading for mercy. The child's plaintive cries were accompanied by the obvious sounds of torture and sexual assault. At the age of 10, the youngest victim was being recorded by the evil couple for their later edification as they put the little girl to death.

The courtroom heard Lesley saying: 'Please take your hands off me a minute, please. Please, Mum, please. I can't tell you. I cannot breathe. Please God. Why? What are you doing with me?' The only other voice was Hindley's, coldly ordering the child to 'shut up', 'come on', 'sit down' and 'be quiet'. The 16-minute tape ended with a scream and a loud cry – and then the sound of a children's favourite song of the time, *The Little Drummer Boy*.

The evidence made the case against Brady and Hindley the most harrowing ever to have come before a British court. The judge said of the killers: 'They are evil beyond belief.' On 6 May, the couple were found guilty of killing Edward Evans and Lesley Ann Downey. In the cases of Pauline Reade and Keith Bennett, the Department of Public Prosecutions decided against a new trial, although both Brady and Hindley had implicated themselves by their statements. Both were given life sentences.

The deviousness of the pair at the time is demonstrated by the fact that, while on remand awaiting trial, Brady and Hindley hatched a plot to escape from prison by exchanging ingenious coded letters from their cells. Police discovered the conspiracy before they could put the plan into operation, ensuring that both prisoners remained a 'high escape risk' after conviction. The escape plan was not revealed to the public until 2008, when confidential documents about the case were released. The papers show that both Brady and Hindley asked to be hypnotised to 'help police' find bodies buried on the Saddleworth Moor. Little Pauline Reade's body was found on the moors in July 1987. Keith Bennett's body still lies there.

During his time in prison, Brady 'confessed' to five other murders, including 'bricking' a man on wasteland behind Manchester's Piccadilly railway station, stabbing a man under railway arches in Glasgow, throwing a woman into a canal in Manchester, shooting and burying an 18-year-old youth on Saddleworth Moor and shooting a hiker at Loch Long, Scotland. But it was difficult to give too much credence to this information from Brady, diagnosed as suffering from a paranoid psychosis. Brady stated that he never wanted to be released and went on prolonged hunger strike in an attempt to end his life, for years being fed forcibly through a tube. Ultimately, he refused to communicate or co-operate with the authorities – one of the few people he corresponded with being forensic psychologist Dr Michael Stone, who placed the killer among 'the worst of the worst' on his expert Scale of Evil.

Myra Hindley, by contrast, campaigned for her release as a totally reformed character and managed to persuade a small band of sympathisers to espouse her cause. The 600 documents released in 2008 included letters to and from her champion, liberal campaigner Lord Longford, who tried to convince the world that Hindley had merely gone along with the murders after falling under Brady's spell. One letter she sent to the peer in 1969 complained about her not being allowed conjugal visits with Brady.

Hindley was wholly unreformed, however. Not mentioned in the files was a 1972 escape attempt she planned in conjunction with a lesbian warder who had fallen for her 'charms'. The killer, who had many lesbian affairs during her imprisonment, was seen by others as a cold, calculating and manipulative woman. She became Britain's longest-serving female prisoner because of her 'whole life' sentence and, after thirty-six years in jail, she died on 15 November 2002, from a chest infection made worse by previous bouts of angina and a stroke. Still reviled because of her crimes against children four decades earlier, her passing still made front-page news. One typical headline read: 'At last Myra is where she belongs – Hell.'

Meanwhile, the suffering of her victims' families continued. Winifred Johnson, whose 12-year-old son Keith Bennett was murdered by Hindley and Brady, pleaded with the pair over the years to identify his moorland grave. One of her letters, sent to Hindley in prison in 1986, read: 'Please, I beg of you, tell me what happened to Keith. My heart tells me you know, and I am on my bended knees begging you to end this torture and finally put my mind at rest.' When she received the letter, Hindley became 'upset and tearful', according to the 2008 files, but the cynical murderess, who, like Brady, had never been convicted of nor had confessed to Keith's killing, claimed that she still had no idea what had happened to the boy.

Mrs Johnson said in 2008: 'Hindley lied then and Brady continues to lie, claiming he doesn't know where Keith is. They felt lying gave them power over me and I hate them for it. I was upset when Hindley died because I wanted her to go on suffering like I have all these years. I hope they burn in hell.'

CHAPTER 21

Randy Kraft

Sexual mutilation was sick trademark of the 'Scorecard Killer'

It was past midnight on a warm Californian night in May 1983. Two Orange County Highway Patrol officers were cruising the quiet streets when they spotted a car being driven erratically. Suspecting the driver of being drunk, they pulled him over, stepped out of their police vehicle and walked towards him. But rather than stay in his own car, as is normally the case, the suspect driver also got out and strolled back towards the officers with a smile on his face. He gave his name as Randy Kraft and said he was a computer engineer on a business trip. Still suspicious, the cops walked him back to his car.

That was the moment when a routine motoring offence became a murder case of horrific proportions. For in Kraft's passenger seat was a body. The corpse, it was later established, was that of Terry Gambrel, a 25-year-old Marine, who had died either of strangulation or an overdose of drugs. Also in the car was a briefcase containing a notebook cataloguing Kraft's sexual encounters and forty-seven photographs of young men, some naked, some dead.

The epithets applied to Randy Kraft when arrested that night, 14 May 1983, included the 'Scorecard Killer' and the 'Freeway Killer'. Another was 'California's worst-ever serial killer', because Kraft's case stands out among the spate of slayings at that time – in that he probably accounted for as many as sixty-seven murders.

Another reason why Kraft stands out from most other serial killers is that he enjoyed a highly successful business career. An IT expert, he travelled America's West Coast and elsewhere, sorting out companies' technology problems and earning himself a large salary which in 1980 amounted to over $50,000 a

year. It was on these business journeys that Kraft, a homosexual, picked up partners and murdered them.

What also became extraordinary about the Kraft case is the
length to which the killer went to avoid justice. By adroit legal
manoeuvring, he delayed his trial for five years, made it drag on
for a record thirteen months at a cost of $ multi-millions, and
further delayed his death sentence by prolonging his stay on
Death Row.

Randy Steven Kraft was born on 19 March 1945, shortly
after his parents moved from Wyoming to Westminster, California. He was a star pupil at Westminster High School, where
he graduated in 1963, and at his college, at Claremont, where
he joined the Reserve Officer Training Corps. There, unlike
many of his peers, he demonstrated in support of the Vietnam
War, and in 1964 campaigned for right-wing presidential can-
didate Barry Goldwater. The following year, he began working
as a bartender at a local gay club. He nevertheless managed
to find time to earn a degree in economics and to continue
political campaigning – although by now his political views had
shifted to the left, and he began working for Robert Kennedy's
political campaign.

Kraft joined the US Air Force in 1968 but was discharged
only a year later on undisclosed medical grounds. He went back
to bartending for a while, but finally put his especially high IQ
of 129 to use by training in computer technology, which he
mastered with ease. He went on to forge for himself a successful
career, with a commensurately large salary, as a sought-after
trouble-shooter for companies' technology problems.

Kraft used these business trips up and down the Pacific Coast
for another purpose, however – picking up homosexual partners
and murdering them. For the next dozen years, the bodies of
Kraft's victims turned up along the freeways of California and
Oregon. The victims were young men and teenage boys. Many
were in the military, hitch-hiking their way between homes and
bases. Some were teenage runaways. Others were picked up by
the killer in gay bars.

It is believed that Kraft claimed his first victim in September
1971. The decomposing body of Wayne Dukette, a 30-year-
old gay barman, was found beside a highway near San Juan
Capistrano. His first confirmed victim, however, was Edward

Moore, a 20-year-old Marine whose body was found near Seal Beach, California, in December 1972. He had been strangled and sexually assaulted. He had been spared sexual mutilation – a perversion that was increasingly to become Kraft's sickening trademark.

Kraft's method of despatching his victims varied. They died of strangulation, were shot in the head or succumbed to torture. Most of the bodies showed signs of sexual mutilation by a sadistic killer. Victims who died in this way, and whose murders were firmly attributed to Kraft, included three in 1975, another in 1976, the victim on this occasion being castrated, four in 1978 and two in 1980. In 1983, no fewer than three Marines were found strangled and mutilated. It was later established that some of his victims had been alive and conscious while Kraft hacked at their genitals.

Because of the number of seemingly random murders along California's highways at the time – contemporaries included Patrick Kearney the 'Trash Bag Killer', Lawrence 'Pliers' Bittaker, Douglas 'Sunset Strip Slayer' Clark and William Bonin, also nicknamed the 'Freeway Killer' – the extent of Kraft's murderous rampage was only realised when he was stopped by the Orange County officers in May 1983. The media gave him his 'Scorecard Killer' tag when police revealed the contents of the briefcase found in his car alongside the body of US Marine Terry Gambrel. In the briefcase was a note-book with the killer's own detailed account of his murders – his 'scorecard'. It gave names, places, how the victims were murdered and the mutilations carried out.

Police were able to decipher the notebook's coded entries, which appeared to show that Kraft had killed both singly and sometimes with an unnamed partner. They also identified many – but not all – of the forty-seven photographs of young men found in the briefcase. More than twenty on the death list remain a mystery to this day but others allowed detectives to piece together the last hours of a number of confirmed victims.

In July 1980, Kraft killed a 17-year-old hitch-hiker, Michael O'Fallon. Although he had overdosed on drugs and alcohol, his death had been caused by strangulation. Bound with his own shoelaces, he had also been tortured with a cord knotted round his scrotum. His body was found dumped beside Interstate 5 near Salem, Oregon. Another 17-year-old hitch-hiker, Michael Cluck, was dumped along the same highway near Goshen, Oregon, in April 1981. He had been beaten to death after being sodomised.

In July 1981, two young victims were found in a ditch beside the Hollywood Freeway, Los Angeles. They were identified as Robert Avila, aged 16, and Raymond Davis, aged only 13. The following month, 17-year-old Christopher Williams was found dead in the San Bernardino Mountains; he had been drugged and had then had paper stuffed up his nostrils to suffocate him.

The killer was back working in Oregon the following year. In November 1982, the body of Brian Whitcher, 26, was found near the I-5 outside Portland. He had been strangled. Kraft's next assignment was in Michigan, where he arrived the following month for a computer conference. In his hotel bar in Grand Rapids, he struck up a conversation with cousins Dennis Alt and Chris Schoenborn. Their bodies were found together in Plainfield Township two days later, both drugged and strangled. Alt's trousers had been pulled down to expose his genitals. Schoenborn was completely nude, a ballpoint pen with the hotel logo on it stuck through his penis and into his bladder.

By the time the cousins' bodies were discovered, Kraft had returned to Oregon and had murdered again. The body of 19-year-old Lance Taggs was dumped close to the spot where Brian Whitcher had been found. He had been doped with valium and had a sock forced down his throat until he choked to death. Kraft's murderous pace was speeding up, for that same month another victim was discovered at the roadside near Hubbard, Oregon. Hitch-hiker Anthony Silveira, 29, had been strangled, brutally sodomised and left with a plastic toothbrush in his anus.

Back in California in January 1983, Kraft drugged, sodomised and battered to death 21-year-old hitch-hiker Eric Church and dumped his body beside the 605 Freeway. His next victim was hitch-hiker Mikael Laine, 24, abducted near Ramona, Orange County. In February, the bodies of 18-year-old Geoffrey Nelson and 20-year-old Roger de Vaul were found in the same area.

All of these young men were listed in the incriminating notebook cataloguing Kraft's sex partners over the years, and most of them were among the forty-seven photographs of his sexual conquests, some of the pictures taken after he had murdered them. One of the victims had not even been listed by police as a homicide case. The body of a 19-year-old Marine, Robert Loggins, had been discovered near California's El Toro airbase in September 1980. A blood sample revealed a deadly level of alcohol and prescription drugs. But since Loggins had recently been confined to barracks for drunkenness, his death was logged as 'accidental'.

However, following Kraft's arrest thirty-two months later, police had in their possession a photograph of Loggins lying naked and dead on a couch in Kraft's home. In a search of the house, in Huntington Beach, police found property and fibres that led them to believe that, apart from the slayings in California, Oregon and Michigan, Kraft had also killed on business trips to Ohio, Washington and New York.

Kraft was charged with sixteen homicides. He confessed to none of them and, by manipulating the legal system, managed to delay his trial for five years. He stretched the hearings out over thirteen months, running up a bill for the Orange County trial of $10 million. In May 1989 he was convicted on all counts – although it took a further four months of legal manoeuvring before sentencing could be ordered and another three months before the jury's formal recommendation. However, time finally ran out for Kraft on 29 November 1989, when he was sentenced to death.

Thereafter, he remained on San Quentin's Death Row, raising a string of appeals to delay justice and absurd litigations to mock the judicial system. One legal challenge he instituted was based on his claim that the gas chamber violated the US Constitution's religious principles by forcing someone to 'actively participate in his own killing'. Another failed lawsuit was a $60 million libel action against an author whose book, he claimed, had portrayed him as a 'sick, twisted man', thereby harming his 'prospects for future employment'. The litigious serial killer had the cell door firmly shut on him when the California Supreme Court upheld his death sentence on 11 August 2000.

Mysteries remain, however, over some aspects of the case. Of Kraft's suspected sixty-seven victims, twenty-two bodies remain unrecovered and unidentified. Another mystery prosecutors could not solve was the question as to whether Kraft had always acted alone. Forensic evidence in two of the murders pointed to an accomplice: an extra set of footprints and semen that did not match Kraft's DNA. Prosecutors believed that the partner who shared Kraft's Huntington Beach home at the time of his arrest, Jeff Graves, had helped him carry out or cover up the killings. Graves died of AIDS before police could question him.

The other tragic question is: why was Kraft not stopped earlier in his murderous career? In 1975, the severed head of 19-year-old Keith Crotwell was found near the Marina at Long Beach, California. He had last been seen a month earlier hitchhiking in the area and being given a lift in a car, the licence plate of which was quickly traced to Kraft. On 19 May 1975, police questioned Kraft, who admitted giving Crotwell a ride but said he dropped him off at an all-night café. Detectives disbelieved him and prepared to charge Kraft with murder. Because of the lack of a complete corpse, however, Los Angeles County prosecutors refused to proceed against the serial killer – condemning dozens more victims to death at the hands of Randy Steven Kraft.

Chapter 22

Leonard Lake & Charles Ng

'Snuff movies' sideline of the killers who filmed victims' agony

I t was just another day, just another shoplifter. The California sun, a great golden globe in an azure sky, dripped lethargy on an already drowsy Sunday city. The only cloud in sight was rising over the eerie island fortress of Alcatraz, then gently settling to engulf the old prison like a wispy shroud. Two tired cops in their battered squad car were planning where to go for a meal break when the call came in: a Chinese man had been seen walking out of a South San Francisco hardware store with a vice he had not paid for.

'More paperwork,' groaned one. 'And the court will just let him off with a caution,' sighed the other. The eternal grumbles of police everywhere. They could not have known that the shoplifter, Charles Ng, was shortly to become America's most wanted man, nor that as a result of this simple, bungled theft attempt they would stumble on one of the most macabre cases of mass murder in the annals of violent California crime.

All this was in the future, however, as the police drove into the store car park where a bearded man in a car was arguing with shop staff. The Chinese man they were expecting to find had been apprehended as he had tried to put the vice in the car boot, but in the ensuing confusion had made good his escape. The cops had then turned their attention to the bearded man who had been with him.

At first he swore that the runaway Chinese man thought he had paid for the vice, then offered to pay the $75 himself. But the stolen vice quickly paled into insignificance when the officers looked into a holdall that was lying in the boot. They found a handgun with a silencer. The cops immediately drew their own weapons and the bearded man was shackled and shaken down. His driving licence gave his name as Robin Scott

Stapley. It was an alias. When a check call was made to the station, the computer revealed that Stapley was a 26-year-old who had disappeared without trace some months previously. The name was on record because shortly after his disappearance, his truck had been involved in a slight accident. It was being driven by a young Chinese man ...

A further computer check on the car in the hardware store car park revealed it was registered to one Paul Cosner, another missing person, who had last been seen by his girlfriend some weeks previously. He had told her he was on his way to sell the car to a 'weird-looking' man who was prepared to pay cash.

It was enough for the police. The bearded man was taken to headquarters. Yet to unfold were the grisly, stomach-churning details of a series of crimes so cold-blooded that case-hardened detectives would grow pale and retch.

At the station, the man was calm. He asked for a glass of water and a pencil and paper to write out a statement. But when he was alone, he calmly took the cyanide pill that he always carried with him, washed it down with the water and scribbled a note to his ex-wife, a dubious character called Claralyn 'Cricket' Balasz. It read: 'I love you. Please forgive me. I forgive you. Tell Mama, Fern and Patty I'm sorry.' Then he called the detectives back, revealed that his real name was Leonard Lake – and fell forward unconscious. He never came round and died four days later.

In Lake's pockets were bills made out to Charles Gunnar, with an address at Wilseyville, in Calaveras County, about 150 miles north of San Francisco. The local sheriff, Claude Ballard, confirmed that Gunnar owned a small ranch in the area which he shared with a young oriental. He also confirmed that the man he knew as Gunnar was, in fact, Lake.

Sheriff Ballard had been taking an interest in the ranch because Lake advertised furniture and TV sets for sale on a regular basis. He had thought some of the articles might be stolen property. Ballard recalled that what had first drawn his attention to the ranch was the sale of furniture of a couple called Lonny Bond and Brenda O'Connor. Lonny and Brenda had been neighbours of Lake, but they had suddenly disappeared without trace, as had their 6-month-old baby, Lonny Junior.

Lake had claimed they had left him their furniture to settle a debt.

In the light of the new information Ballard received from San Francisco, he recalled another mystery disappearance from a local camp site, when a couple vanished leaving their tent and equipment, with even a pot of coffee boiling on the stove.

Hackles rising, officers prepared to raid Lake's home on Blue Mountain Road in rural, wooded Wilseyville. The two-bedroom cabin was set in three acres. From outside it seemed idyllic. But they were sickened by what they found. In the master bedroom they saw hooks in the ceiling and walls and in a box they found shackles. They had stumbled upon a torture chamber. Inside a wardrobe they found women's underwear and flimsy nightgowns. In the yard they found charred bones that looked human. But the worst horror was still to unfold.

Dug securely into the hillside near the cabin was a bomb-proof and well-concealed bunker. Lake, a former Marine who had been drummed out of the service on psychiatric grounds, believed that World War III was about to break out, and in his warped mind he saw himself as the kind of man who should survive. The bunker was provided with all amenities and stocked with food to see him through the coming holocaust. In the meantime, it served to fulfil his other fantasy: that of domination over women. It was also, it transpired, the centre of a perverted business empire based on his cruel, warped fantasies. As well as sleeping, living and toilet facilities, there were other rooms that looked for all the world like prison cells, complete with shackles and leg-irons. There were also pictures adorning the walls of naked and semi-clad women. Some of the pictures appeared to be of newly-dead corpses, their faces twisted in pain.

With the principal character dead and his accomplice on the run, the police took the place apart in an effort to uncover the grim truth. They already feared the worst, but even so, they were not prepared for what they were to find. In a cabinet were full records of Lake's twisted career, on film, in pictures and in two 500-page journals in his own hand ...

Leonard Lake was born into a poor family on 29 October 1945 in San Francisco, where he died by his own hand on 6 June 1985. In the thirty-nine-and-a-half years of his perverted life, he had been a trader, teacher, fireman, Marine and circus showman. He had also been a drugs dealer and the director and co-star in his own 'snuff' videos: pornographic home movies in which the victim, almost invariably a woman or a child, is subjected to sadistic sexual practices or ritual torture and, as a climax, is killed while the camera lingers over the gruesome, graphic detail. Lake had not just satisfied his bloodlust, he had made a lucrative income from it.

At last, all was revealed in Lake's own video library. Shocked police who viewed the films took it in turns to leave the room as one after the other became sickened by what he saw. One film, labelled only 'M Ladies Kathy/Brenda' opens with a young woman, hands cuffed behind her back, sitting on a chair in the cabin. A voice off-camera tells her: 'Mike owes us and he can't pay. We're going to give you a choice, Kathy.' The menacing, disembodied voice continues: 'You can co-operate and in approximately thirty days we'll either drug you or blindfold you and let you go somewhere in the city. If you don't co-operate, we'll put a bullet in your head and bury you some place. No witnesses. While you're here, you'll wash for us, you'll clean for us, you'll fuck for us. That's your choice. It's not much of a choice unless you have a death wish.'

Lake, heavy-set, bearded and balding, then comes into view to put leg-irons on Kathy. 'My name you don't know,' he tells her, then adds, 'it is Charlie.' As he speaks these words, another man enters the frame. It is Ng – the Chinese man who in-advertently set the investigation in motion with his bungled attempt to steal a $75 vice. Lake removes the handcuffs and orders Kathy to strip. The woman, later identified as missing person Kathy Allen, removes her outer clothes and her bra, but is reluctant to take off her panties until Ng points to the gun on the table. Finally, shaking and crying, she strips naked and is sent to take a shower with Ng.

A later scene in the video has Kathy strapped, still naked, to a bed. It is four days later and Lake is threatening her as he takes pornographic photographs. He tells her that Mike (her boy-friend) is now dead, and soon it will be her turn.

The scene shifts back to the cabin, where a young woman called Brenda sits shackled on a chair as Kathy did before her. Beside Brenda, holding a vicious-looking knife, stands Ng. As

Lake gives Brenda the same instructions he gave Kathy, Ng uses the knife to cut away Brenda's blouse. This time, though, the threats carry more menace. Lake tells Brenda that her baby has been given to a family in Fresno. She becomes hysterical and begs for the return of the child. Lake and Ng laugh.

'Why do you guys do this?' she asks plaintively.

'We don't like you,' says Lake.

As Ng removes the shreds of her blouse she pleads: 'Don't cut my bra off.'

'Nothing is yours now,' says Lake.

'Give me back my baby. I'll do anything you want.'

'You'll do anything we want anyway.'

Ng slowly cuts away the woman's bra. At last the sickening tape comes to an end. It was the last that was ever seen of Kathy Allen and Brenda O'Connor. Their remains were subsequently found with those of nineteen others in shallow trenches near the cabin. Also found were the teeth of Lonny Junior – the child Brenda had pleaded so desperately for.

It was not the only film police had to sweat through as their rage and frustration mounted. There was a collection of films depicting all manner of ritual tortures, rapes and degrading sex acts. And many of them culminated in the horror of real on-screen murder. These, along with a lucrative drug-trafficking sideline, were the basis of Lake's income. There were also pictures of naked women in chains, pictures of dead bodies, their faces frozen in the agony of death. And there were bags of human bones which had been boiled down to a soup.

In Lake's journal, investigators read: 'The perfect woman is totally controlled, a woman who does exactly what she is told and nothing else. There is no sexual problem with a submissive woman. There are no frustrations, only pleasure and content-ment.'

What could explain Leonard Lake's macabre fixation with wanton murder along with the subjugation and degradation of women? Lake's family had a history of mental disorders and alcoholism. At the age of 6, poverty forced his parents to send him to live with his grandparents, where he received a tough, militaristic upbringing. Meanwhile his younger brother Donald, an epileptic, remained at home, becoming something of a mother's boy. But despite the attention he received from her, he developed a cruel streak that he exercised on animals – and on his sisters. He started setting fires and had he not himself been murdered, as we shall see, he might also have become a serial killer.

Donald tried to tape his sisters on numerous occasions. Lake was asked by them for protection and in turn demanded – and received – sexual favours. His interest in the nude female body began in late childhood and, incredibly, his grandmother encouraged him to take photographs of naked girls, including his sisters and cousins.

As a youngster, he was obsessive. He studied and experimented with pet mice, tracing genetic features through numerous generations. Through such single-mindedness, he became a self-taught geneticist. He also had a compulsion for cleanliness, washing and showering many times a day. In his torture videos, the victim was always made to shower before the degrading and bloody action began in earnest.

Leonard Lake lived in a world of fantasy, dreaming of Vikings, Valhalla and stirring adventure. In 1965 he joined the Marine Corps, and later boasted of his deeds in Vietnam – but in reality he had never seen combat. During his service, he spent two years undergoing psychiatric treatment for unspecified mental problems before his discharge in 1971. He then moved to San Jose, California, and had a short-lived first marriage. Lake was known to be making porn films featuring his wife and several other women at that time.

Lake found work as a grade school teacher and circus showman. He was one of a team that created a 'unicorn', grafting a single horn on the head of a goat. Later he was the barker for the attraction at a sideshow belonging to Barnum and Bailey. However, another employee recalled later walking into his motel room and seeing a large pot boiling on the stove. When he lifted the lid, he found the head of a single-horned goat boiling into soup. In 1981 he moved to rural Ukiah, California, joining a commune whose residents dressed in 'Renaissance'-style clothing and led bizarre lives. While living at the commune, he married Cricket Balasz, who became another star of his sadomasochistic films.

This, then, was the background of the man whose home police were searching following his suicide in June 1985. While officers continued to uncover grisly discoveries at the woodland hideaway, others ran a fingerprint check that showed Lake (under yet another name) was wanted in Humboldt County for jumping bail on charges of burglary. Following up, local sheriffs discovered that hey had started to build another survivalist bolt-hole, and the found maps with marks pointing to 'hidden treasure'. These too turned out to be the graves of his victims.

One of these was none other than his own brother, Donald. He had visited Lake to try to get some money but his elder brother had coolly murdered him. Another grave belonged to the one man who had befriended Lake in the Marines: Charles Gunnar, whose identity Lake assumed. Among the bodies that were dug up were those of two blacks. Ng had been seen driving two black men to the ranch, even though he was known to hate blacks and Hispanics. One further mystery seemed to have been solved: that of a San Francisco couple, Harvey and Deborah Dubs, who had disappeared along with their baby. A policeman recalled seeing a Chinese man moving furniture out of their home. By coincidence, the same policeman was now working on the Lake-Ng case.

Attention now focussed on the escaped Ng, and police delved into his background, which was almost totally the reverse of Lake's. Charles Chi-Tat Ng was born in 1960, the son of a wealthy Hong Kong-based businessman. When, at the age of 15, Charles was caught shoplifting, his parents sent him to an English boarding school in Yorkshire, from where he was expelled for theft. For a time, he lived in Preston, Lancashire, until he was sent to San Francisco to complete his education.

At 18, he was involved in a hit-and-run traffic accident and joined the Marines to escape arrest. Never in his life short of money, he was evidently a kleptomaniac and was soon arrested at Kaneoke Air Force base in Oahu, Hawaii. The charge was stealing weapons worth $11,000. Sentenced to twenty-seven months in a military jail, he managed to escape and made his way back to San Francisco, where he applied to an advertisement in a survivalist magazine for a 'mercenary'.

The advert had been placed by Lake, who was himself a 'survivalist' and believed the 'holocaust' was coming. He had constructed a sick fantasy in his mind that he labelled

'Operation Miranda', where he saw himself in total world domination surrounded by his 'sex-slaves'.

When Lake, then aged 37, and Ng, aged 21, met up in 1982, a barbarous partnership was forged. Their evil business plans had to be put on hold when the pair were picked up on a burglary charge in Humboldt County and Ng, identified as a deserter, served time at Fort Leavenworth, Kansas. Soon out on parole, however, he returned to Lake in California – and the pair embarked on their three-year killing spree.

Now, with his partner dead, Ng had become the FBI's most wanted man. The first lead to his whereabouts came a few days after the raid on the cabin, when a San Francisco gun dealer rang the police to say that Ng had phoned him about a gun he was repairing. He had asked the dealer to post it to Chicago and when it was explained to him that it was against the law to mail guns across state lines, Ng had cursed and rung off.

In July 1985, five weeks after Lake was seized, Ng was seen stealing from a store in Calgary, Canada. When challenged, he pulled a gun and shot a security man in the hand. As more guards arrived on the scene, Ng showed he was adept at martial arts but eventually he was overpowered. When FBI agents arrived in Canada to interview Ng, he told them he knew of the murders but had played no part in them. He was, however, able to describe the murders of Paul Cosner, whose car had been found in Lake's possession, and of two removal men, one of whom was burned to death.

A Canadian court sentenced Ng to four and a half years for armed robbery, although it at first refused to agree to extradition proceedings, on the grounds that California still maintained the death penalty. After a long extradition battle, Ng was finally handed over to the US authorities and convicted of eleven murders, the victims being six men, three women and two babies. The trial was one of the longest and most expensive in Californian history. He was sentenced to death on 30 June 1999, and is languishing on Death Row in San Quentin State Prison, where he has submitted a string of appeals in his attempt to beat the might of the American legal system.

As American serial killers go, Leonard Lake and Charles Ng were not record breakers. The toll of their victims numbered probably between thirty and forty. What makes Leonard Lake, in particular, a unique example in the annals of serial killer crime is the way he turned the bloodlust that drove him to kill neighbours, friends – even his own brother – into an efficient and well-organised business. Adverts offering to buy or sell various goods were the lure to get people to the cabin. They never left alive. Film of their torture and appalling deaths, however, fed the fantasies of perverts across the nation and beyond.

And yet, all the time, the outside world saw him as a thoroughly nice guy. To outsiders and even close members of his family, Lake was a model citizen, a volunteer firefighter and a charity worker with the elderly. In fact, his cover was perfect. Following the revelations of his vile trade in torture and death, relatives were reluctant to talk, though his ex-wife Cricket Balasz was a little more forthcoming. She was not surprised to hear of her ex-husband's snuff video operation. He had been making porno videos while they were married – and she had been the star. Her role had been to act out various sado-masochistic roles, as she mouthed the name of the client. She had wondered at the time whether he was making other, weirder films on the side.

Even after the damning evidence was laid bare, his mother, a nurse who worked in a mental hospital, could not believe her son was capable of violence. His sister Fern, also a nurse, had always looked the other way, while his grandmother would hear no ill of her darling Leonard, insisting he was a good child who had been led astray. It was left to a man who had lived with Lake in a commune a few years before his death to sum up the pornographer and mass-murderer behind the mask of a neighbourly charity volunteer. Lake was, he said, 'the pleasant-est unpleasant guy you ever could meet'.

CHAPTER 23

Robert Pickton

Girls lured to parties at pig farm that became a charnel house

It is officially the poorest neighbourhood in the whole of Canada. Vancouver's Downtown Eastside is the ugly part of the beautiful province of British Columbia that the tourists do not see. It encompasses ten blocks of squalor, home to drunks, drug addicts and the mentally unstable.

The ghetto's junkie population is estimated at between 5,000 and 10,000. But it is the sad array of prostitutes that is at the core of the 'economy' of this area that the locals refer to as, simply, 'Low Track'. Some of these hookers, many below the age of consent, simply vanish. Few people notice.

That is how an evil pig farmer named Robert 'Willie' Pickton got away with murder for so long. Largely due to AIDS, the life expectancy in Downtown Eastside is less than forty. But when Pickton was operating there, it became dramatically lower for his victims, mainly prostitutes and drug addicts from Canada's poorest postcode.

Pickton, born in British Columbia on 24 October 1949, was well-known for the parties he threw for prostitutes, junkies and bikers. He lured the women to his 16-acre pig farm in Port Coquitlam, just outside Vancouver, with the promise of money and drugs. Pickton then killed them and disposed of their remains by feeding them to his pigs.

In a contested confession, Pickton ultimately confessed to murdering some forty-nine women, although he was only ever charged with six homicides. The women, who disappeared between 1997 and 2001, were those for whom adequate body parts survived for cases to be brought against him.

The trail began to lead to Pickton's pig farm only in 1998, and only because of the persistence of two loving parents.

Following the sudden disappearance of heroin addict Marnie Frey, her father and stepmother took matters into their own hands and mounted a search for their daughter on the streets of Downtown Eastside. What they were to uncover shocked them – and not least the attitude of the Vancouver police.

For the couple became convinced, after talking to drug addicts and prostitutes, that a serial killer was on the prowl. As Mrs Lynn Frey reported to a newspaper: 'The girls told me, "There's this guy who picks up girls in vans and takes them to a farm and they don't come back." That's as much as they'd tell me – then they'd run away scared and wouldn't say any more.'

The Freys found support from out of the neighbourhood for their search, and support from within for the accusation that police lacked concern for the many missing women who had disappeared from the ghetto over the course of twenty years. From the police, however, they encountered an adamant refusal to believe that a serial killer was at large.

Even at this stage, the finger of suspicion had fallen on Robert Pickton. Mrs Frey's sister knew of the scruffy pig farm where Pickton lived, and Mrs Frey vainly passed his name to detectives as a suspect. When the police failed to act, the local press launched its own campaign.

The breakthrough came with a call to *The Vancouver Sun* from Bill Hiscox, a former employee on the Pickton farm. He knew a woman who had been inside the trailer where Mr Pickton lived. 'She doesn't want to get involved – she's kind of scared about it,' Hiscox was recorded as saying on tape. 'But she told me, "Billy, you wouldn't believe the IDs and s*** in that trailer. There's women's clothes out there, there's purses. You know, what's that guy doing? It's, like, really weird."'

The newspaper passed this evidence to the police but it wasn't until four years later, in February 2002, that officers raided the pig farm in an unrelated investigation into illegal firearms, reported by an ex-employee, Scott Chubb. During their search, police stumbled upon an asthma inhaler prescribed in the name of one of the missing women and the ID cards of several others. They returned with another warrant and began searching the property, beginning with the slaughterhouse.

Investigators dug up the remains of one woman after another, from body parts to minute traces of DNA, until the count came to thirty. Four could not be identified. The other twenty-six were among the names of sixty-seven women who had disappeared from the Downtown Eastside streets.

In the freezers, investigators found evidence that included skulls of two women among the most recently reported missing. They were cut in half like the carcasses of the slaughtered pigs, their hands and feet stuffed inside. The remains of another victim were in a garbage bag in the bottom of a trash can and her bloodstained clothing was found in the trailer in which Pickton lived. Part of one victim's jawbone and teeth were found in the ground beside the slaughterhouse.

One victim, Sereena Abotsway, had gone missing only a few months after leading a protest march against police inaction over the killings.

Much of the evidence may have been devoured long before police set foot on the farm. In convoluted language, a 2003 police health study reported: 'It is believed that there is a possibility that human remains were fed to pigs but the risk of disease to those who may have had contact with the meat was negligible. The psychological effects may be worse than the physical.'

The case against Pickton relied mainly on one police witness, three civilian witnesses, plus forensic evidence linked to remains found on his property and the trailer where he slept. The first of these witnesses was introduced on the first day of the trial, 22 January 2007, when the prosecution stated that the accused farmer had confessed to forty-nine murders in a conversation with an undercover police officer posing as a cellmate. Pickton had told the officer that he wanted to kill another woman to make it an even fifty, and that he was caught because he was 'sloppy'.

The first civilian witness was Scott Chubb, who testified that Pickton told him the way to get rid of junkies was to inject them with a syringe filled with windshield-washer fluid. A syringe with the liquid had indeed been found in Pickton's trailer.

Another witness who had stayed on the farm told how he received a first-hand demonstration by Pickton of how to murder a woman. Andrew Bellwood testified that Pickton came into his trailer one night and asked him if he wanted to pick up a prostitute in the Downtown Eastside. Bellwood told the court that when he said he wasn't interested, Pickton pulled three items from under the mattress in the room: a pair of handcuffs, a leather belt without a buckle and thin wire with loops on the end. Bellwood said Pickton got on the bed and showed him that he strangled the women while having sex with them.

The third witness, Lynn Ellingsen, told the jury how, after waking up from a crack binge at the farm one night, she had gone outside to the barn because she saw a light on. When she opened the door, she saw a body hanging from a chain. Beside the body was a bloodied Pickton, who warned her that 'she'd be next' if she said anything.

Pickton's was the longest trial in Canadian history. The statistics were mind-boggling, and perhaps explained why the jury found decision-making such a drawn-out task. The forensic labs offered about 600,000 exhibits; 500,000 pages of documents were produced; 235,000 items were seized from the crime scene; 40,000 photographs were taken; ninety-eight witnesses appeared for the prosecution and thirty for the defence, and Pickton's taped interrogation lasted twenty hours.

Given this weight of evidence, it is little wonder that it took the jury of seven men and five women ten days to reach a verdict. In December 2007, Pickton, by then aged 58, received a mandatory life sentence, with no possibility of parole, for the murders of Mona Wilson, Brenda Wolfe, Sereena Abotsway, Andrea Joesbury, Georgina Papin and Marnie Frey.

It was the close of a trial that had seen reporters seeking psychological counselling because of the macabre nature of some of the evidence, and one in which the judge had warned jurors that they were hearing testimony 'as bad as in a horror movie'. But although the trial was ended and it was acknowledged that Pickton was certainly responsible for at least twenty-six murders, the cases of thirty-nine missing women remained open and police scientists continued to sift through samples taken from the farm to find any trace of them.

In a sorry postscript to the case, even after Pickton had been locked up, girls continued to be violated and murdered on the streets of Downtown Eastside – twenty men having been convicted of murdering individual prostitutes in as many years, and one pervert being convicted in 2005 of the sexual assault and tape-recorded torture of nearly sixty prostitutes. None of the sixty had trusted the police sufficiently to report the attacks. Under public pressure following the Pickton trial, Vancouver police held an inquiry into their failings. It was held in private.

CHAPTER 24

David Berkowitz

'I prowl the streets for tasty meat,' wrote 'Son of Sam'

By day, David Berkowitz was a seemingly innocent post office worker, a podgy, cherubic-faced loner who lived quietly in his tiny suburban apartment. By night, he was a fiend, the madman who, in his unearthly alter ego 'Son of Sam', would become the most terrifying and mysterious serial slaughterer ever to stalk New York City. For more than twelve shocking months, beginning in July 1976, the curly-haired killer held the city in a grip of palpable terror as he went gunning for vivacious, attractive victims.

Initially dubbed the '.44 calibre killer' because of the weapon he used in all of his demented attacks, Berkowitz killed six of his victims and severely wounded seven others. Five of those females sought to protect themselves any way they could at the height of the widespread panic when police seemed helpless to stop the carnage. Apart from the random nature of the crimes and the apparent lack of motive, what terrified the city most were the bizarre, twisted letters the 24-year-old Berkowitz would send to police and a newspaper columnist at the peak of his insane rampage. He taunted the police efforts to track him down, warning 'I'll be back' and boasting 'I love to hunt, prowling the streets for fair game, tasty meat.' By July 1977, New York was, according to a newspaper account of the time, 'exploding' – a city under siege from an unknown terror its agencies of law and order seemed powerless to stop.

Berkowitz's first victim was Donna Lauria, a pretty 18-year-old who, keeping a promise to her father not to be too late home, was closing her car door and saying goodnight to her friend Jody Valenti when the killer struck in the early hours of 29 July 1976. Berkowitz had obviously been watching as the two girls sat and chatted outside the neat Bronx apartment of

Donna's parents. He then ran from the shadows, stood on the footpath to Donna's home, pulled his .44 calibre gun from a paper bag, crouched down and fired three shots. Donna died and Jody was wounded.

As far as the cops were concerned, it was just another randomly crazy crime in a city whose murder rate stood at thirty a week. Police were baffled by the senseless killing, but on the violence-soaked streets of New York City that is hardly cause for headlines. Within a few days, Donna Lauria's name had faded from the newspapers, and that was the last anyone save the grieving family thought they would ever hear of the incident.

The unknown assailant would not strike again until 23 October when again the targets were two hapless young people in a parked car, this time at Flushing, Queens. Detective's daughter Rosemary Keenan, 18, escaped the bullets but her friend Carl Denaro, 20, had his plans to enlist the following week in the US Air Force shattered when he was critically wounded in the head. Incredibly, he survived the attack. Even then, no one yet contemplated that New York was in the grip of a serial killer.

Again, police ballistic tests showed the gunman had used a .44 calibre pistol, but it was too early for the alarm bells to ring down at Police Headquarters. New York in the 1970s averaged about thirty killings a week and an already overworked police force failed to notice the similarities in the two incidents: the type of gun, the fact that the victims were young and shot while in parked cars and that the killer struck late at night or early in the morning.

Two more young women were shot and seriously wounded – one to spend the rest of her life in a wheelchair – when the mysterious gunman surfaced again on 26 November. The pair were sitting on the steps of Joanne Lomino's home in Floral Park, Queens, when Berkowitz walked up and shot them both. Joanne Lomino was wounded and recovered but Donna DeMasi, with a bullet in her spine, was permanently paralysed.

In January 1977, John Diel and girlfriend Christine Freund were sitting in their parked car in the Ridgewood district when two bullets shattered the passenger window. Diel was unhurt but his date died later in hospital. Visiting Bulgarian student Virginia Voskerichian was the next victim, shot in the face as she approached her home in Forest Hills one evening in March. The bullet that killed her was found to be from the same .44 calibre pistol as had been used in the previous shootings. Following this discovery, a '.44 Killer' Task Force was organised, although for a long time the 300-strong squad found themselves working in the dark. No motive for the shootings could be deduced because, although the same gun was being used, the victims were totally random.

That all changed with the very next attack on 17 April 1977, when detectives realised they were dealing with a particularly unusual breed of killer. Examining the bodies of student Valentina Suriani and boyfriend Alexander Esau, shot as they sat in their car in the Bronx, police found that their assassin had left more than death in his wake. Berkowitz had planted the first of a series of callously teasing letters – a four-page missive that gave birth to 'Son of Sam'.

In it, the twisted killer wrote that he was 'deeply hurt' about the descriptions in the press which characterised him as a woman-hater. 'I am not,' wrote Berkowitz. 'But I am a monster. I am the Son of Sam. I am a little brat. Sam loves to drink blood. "Go out and kill" commands father Sam . . . I am on a different wavelength to everybody else – programmed to kill. However, to stop me you must kill me. Attention all police: Shoot me first – shoot to kill or else. Keep out of my way or you will die! I am the monster – "Beelzebub, the Chubby Behemoth". I love to hunt. Prowling the streets looking for fair game – tasty meat. I live for the hunt – my life. I don't belong on earth. I'll be back! I'll be back! Yours in murder – Mr Monster.'

The authorities decided against publicising the letter, though some parts of it were eventually leaked to the newspapers. But on 30 May, the killer, hoping to heighten the terror, changed his tactics, this time by writing directly to Jimmy Breslin, a well-known and highly-respected columnist on the *New York Daily News*. The letter, even more nightmarish than the first one, was published in the following day's edition, and sent the city into the fearful panic 'Son of Sam' had craved.

It began: 'Hello from the gutters of NYC, which are filled with dog manure, vomit, stale wine, urine and blood. Hello from the sewers of NYC which swallow up these delicacies when they are washed away by the sweeper trucks. Hello from the cracks in the sidewalks of NYC and from the ants that dwell in these cracks and feed on the dried blood of the dead that has seeped into these cracks.'

The killer ominously warned Breslin that he had not yet finished his 'work'. 'Mr Breslin, sir, don't think that because you haven't heard from (me) for a while that I went to sleep. No, rather, I am still here. Like a spirit roaming the night. Thirsty, hungry, seldom stopping to rest.'

But who was this 'Mr Monster'? David Berkowitz was born illegitimately in Brooklyn on 1 June 1953. His name at birth was Richard David Falco, his 39-year-old mother Betty being an ex-chorus girl who had once performed with the famous Ziegfeld Follies. Betty had been deserted by her husband thirteen years before David was born and was having a long-term affair with a Long Island businessman at the time. He ordered her to get rid of the child and she did.

Although the young David knew little or nothing of his real mother and father, he was fortunate enough to be raised by caring, adoptive parents Nathan and Pearl Berkowitz, who ran a hardware store in the Bronx. He was to be their only child. Of above-average intelligence, David was reasonably popular at school and was good at sport but he was a habitual truant, feigning sickness to stay at home with his doting mother. He was deeply affected when Pearl Berkowitz died in his early teens. He complained that her death was 'part of a masterplan to break me down', adding: 'It was no accident that she got cancer. Evil forces put something in her food.' He once wrote of his self-pitying teenage days: 'I begged God for death. I used to sit on the fire escape and thought of throwing myself down, wanting to jump. When I thought about dying, I thought about being transported into a world of bliss and happiness.'

When he was 18, his adoptive father remarried and the dis-approving David left home. He enlisted in the US Army, serving in Korea. His three years of service life were unremark-able, except for being brought up on a few minor disciplinary charges and his dramatic conversion from Judaism to funda-mentalist Christianity. Indeed, so complete was the change that Berkowitz often tried to convert fellow soldiers and residents of Louisville, Kentucky, where he was stationed. Off duty, he would preach from street corners, warning of 'the burning fires of Hell that lie in wait for all sinners'.

In the spring of 1974, Berkowitz returned to New York and rented a small apartment in his native Bronx. It was shortly after his return to civilian life that the events began to unfold that would eventually help turn the religious, tubby Berkowitz into the madness of 'Son of Sam'. Firstly, his father, from whom he had been estranged for some time since his conversion to Christianity, quit New York for retirement in Florida, leaving David with a terrible sense of longing. Next, his search to find his real mother came to a numbing conclusion when he discovered that he was illegitimate, and that his mother had a daughter, Roslyn, whom she had not put up for adoption.

These events left Berkowitz a brooding, disillusioned drifter, with few friends or family to stop his slide into a perverted fantasy land. By February 1976, five months before he would begin the slaughter, he moved from his Bronx home to nearby New Rochelle, but after just two months he abruptly changed addresses again, to Yonkers, some 25 miles north of the city.

After a spell as a security guard, he joined the US Mail, sorting letters. In a twisted irony, the quiet postal worker may even have personally overseen, through New York's mail system, the chilling notes he wrote and sent giving tantalising clues to his identity as one of America's most publicised serial killers.

As he sorted the mail, Berkowitz's perverted fantasies grew – until he put them into bloody practice in the summer of 1976. As his crimes became recognised as the work of a serial killer, the chubby mailman craved even greater recognition. After first taunting the New York Police Department, he extended his letter-writing by sending notes to the *New York Post* and the *New York Daily News*. Soon the newspapers and the police came to dread the psychopathic scrawl that was dropping through their mailboxes. It meant that 'Son of Sam' had killed again and was planning his next murder. That is when columnist Jimmy Breslin began writing letters back to 'Son of Sam' in the *New York Daily News*. It was a controversially dangerous tactic. But, though horrified that a murdering psychopath was in their midst, New Yorkers could not help but be fascinated by the bizarre communications between the writer and the killer.

Although Breslin described the 'Son of Sam' mail as 'letters from Hell', he responded to them promptly. 'Will you kill again?' Breslin wrote to 'Son of Sam' a year after the first murder. Berkowitz refused to be drawn. He was still sorting mail on 29 July 1977, the anniversary of his first attack, and the date passed uneventfully. Instead, Berkowitz chose the very next night to strike, shooting Stacy Moskowitz and her date, Robert Violante, as they sat in their car on a Brooklyn street. Stacy, 20, died in hospital and her boyfriend was blinded.

New York was now a city under siege. But the reign of terror of 'Son of Sam' was drawing to an end – in the most extraordinary manner. In the days following the Moskowitz murder, Detective James Justis, a veteran member of NYPD recently recruited into the Task Force, telephoned the owners of several cars which had been given parking tickets around the vicinity of the latest death scene, hoping someone might have seen something suspicious. It was a boring, routine part of police work, and no one expected anything dramatic to come of it. But Justis was doggedly persistent, especially in his attempts to contact the owner of a 1970 four-door Galaxie, cream-coloured with a black vinyl roof, which had been ticketed for parking too close to a fire hydrant just thirty minutes before the most recent murder. When Justis found that his repeated telephone calls to the owner went unanswered, he rang the local Yonkers police force to ask them to call on the man, a David Berkowitz.

Justis spoke with Yonkers switchboard operator Wheat Carr – an incredible coincidence given her family's association with the killer, which suddenly came to light. For when Justis mentioned Berkowitz's name, Carr told him: 'He is the guy that I think is responsible.' She went on to describe several bizarre incidents involving Berkowitz, including claims that he had shot her with a .44 calibre gun and had been sending threatening notes to her father, whose name was Sam. An excited Justis immediately reported the conversation to his superiors.

Despite the amazing revelations, his supervisors weren't particularly excited about this latest lead because they had been receiving worthless tips about thousands of suspected 'Sons of Sam' since the Task Force was formed. Still, they realised Berkowitz had to be interviewed, and the following day

Detectives Ed Zigo and John Longo were sent up to suburban Yonkers to seek out this latest suspect.

After locating his apartment building on Pine Street, they spotted his vehicle, licence plate 561XLB, parked about 30 yards down the quiet street and went over to investigate. Through the windows, they saw a rifle butt protruding from a duffel bag in the back seat. They broke into the car and, in the glove box, found an envelope addressed to Timothy Dowd, a deputy inspector leading the 'Son of Sam' Task Force. Zigo opened it and read the enclosed letter, which Berkowitz had intended leaving at the scene of his next shooting. It promised more attacks, including a planned massacre at a Long Island nightclub where Berkowitz planned to 'go out in a blaze of glory'.

New York Police had suddenly found their 'Son of Sam'. A call was made for a search warrant to allow the detectives to enter Berkowitz's apartment – which they would later discover was eerily devoid of furnishings, contained satanic paraphernalia and pornographic magazines, and had a small hole smashed into the wall, through which the 'demons' spoke to him. None of this was yet known, however, because at 10.00pm, before the search warrant had been issued, the night stalker himself emerged from the building. He was dressed in jeans, brown boots and a white short-sleeved shirt, and in his hand was a brown paper bag containing a .44 calibre gun.

Berkowitz sauntered casually to his car, so confident that he didn't bother to look around. He switched on the ignition but got no further. The barrels of fifteen guns were suddenly levelled through the car windows directly at his head. Berkowitz merely smiled, accepting his fate with icy detachment. 'Okay,' he said, 'you've got me. What took you so long?'

Back at Manhattan police headquarters, senior officers excitedly broke the news to Mayor Abe Beame at his official Gracie Mansion residence. Word of Berkowitz's capture had already been leaked to the media, and they besieged One Police Plaza. Six hours after his arrest, the suspect was grilled for two hours, confessing to all of the 'Son of Sam' crimes and revealing a twisted mind that baffled detectives. Berkowitz persistently told them that all the crimes he had committed had been ordered by 'Sam'.

'Who is Sam?' asked Ronald Aiello, head of the homicide bureau at the Brooklyn District Attorney's office.

'My master,' came the reply.

'Do you want to tell me how you got those orders?'

'Yes, he told me through his dog, as he usually does. It's not really a dog. It just looks like a dog. It's not. He just gave me an idea where to go. When I got the word, I didn't know who I would go out to kill – but I would know when I saw the right people.'

The following morning, Berkowitz was arraigned at Brooklyn courthouse. The waiting press and public expected to see a chained, wild-eyed monster but the man led into the building was a still-smiling nonentity looking as dangerous as a lamb. Nevertheless, a mob of several hundred angry citizens chanted 'Kill him! Kill him! Kill him!' and there were numerous telephoned death threats to the switchboard at the institution where he was subsequently taken for psychiatric evaluation.

During his enforced stay at the heavily-guarded Kings County Hospital, Berkowitz underwent many days of psychiatric tests to delve into the mind of this self-confessed monster. The killer had long been uncomfortable in female company and believed that women avoided him and thought him ugly. 'There is a force to turn people away from me,' he once wrote. 'Somebody wants me destroyed, makes people dislike me and makes girls be not attracted to me in any way. If I had close friends or girlfriends, I would be able to resist the force.'

Still a virgin when arrested, he revealed that he had tried to kill two women in random knife attacks in 1975, a full year before his first shooting. His would-be victims had saved themselves by screaming as they fought him off. Tellingly, Berkowitz said later: 'I didn't want to hurt them. I only wanted to kill them.'

Berkowitz told a criminal psychiatrist: 'The tension, the desire to kill a woman had built up in me to such explosive proportions that when I finally pulled the trigger, all the pressures, all the tensions, hatred, had just vanished, disappeared.' He added that after killing one young woman, 'I was literally singing to myself on the way home.' Psychiatrist Dr David Abrahamsen, who examined Berkowitz and judged him sane, said of him: 'He found sexual gratification in killing women. He could not approach a woman as a man would do and date her or have sex with her. That was not for him. I think he developed a great deal of contempt for women. He is very dangerous.'

While in Kings County Hospital, Berkowitz responded to a letter smuggled to him from Steve Dunleavy, a columnist with the *New York Post*. The reply to Dunleavy was chilling. It spoke of Sam as 'one of the devils of Satan, a force beyond the wildest imaginations of people. He is not human'. It continued: 'When I killed, I really saved many lives. You will understand later. People want my blood but they don't want to listen to what I have to say. There are other Sons out there. God help the world.'

This still did not answer the question: Who is 'Son of Sam'? Bizarrely, the explanation seemed to be that Sam was a neighbour, Sam Carr, whose dog kept him awake at night with its barking. The dog, a black labrador, would howl as Berkowitz lay in bed in his squalid apartment, dreaming of the occult and listening to 'voices' that ordered him to kill. Berkowitz said he had tried to kill the dog in 1977 but demons deflected his bullet and the wounded animal recovered. He had only managed to increase the volume of the animal's nightly barking. Police who searched the apartment found the walls covered with scrawled slogans, the most common being: 'Kill for my master.'

So, was Berkowitz as insane as he sounded? Any thought of a defence plea of insanity was forestalled by the accused pleading guilty to all charges. On 23 August 1977, he was sentenced to 365 years, to be served at the Attica Correctional Facility. There, in July 1979, Son of Sam almost died after a fellow inmate slashed his throat with a razor, the wound requiring fifty-six stitches. The chubby mailman doggedly refused to name his attacker.

Berkowitz also remained tight-lipped about conspiracy theories raised over the years by private investigators, writers and law enforcement officials that he did not act alone. In an interview two months after his capture, Berkowitz hinted that he was not the lone gunman, but that he didn't want to expose the details because he was scared of what might happen to his family. He claimed he was protecting 'hundreds of people' and that they were continuing with the killings which police were 'absolutely powerless' to stop.

It was in part due to the declaration that 'other' depraved killers like him were loose that has led some to suspect that Berkowitz was part of a demonic cult. The varied descriptions given by witnesses of strangers at the scenes of Berkowitz's crimes gave this theory some credence. And Berkowitz's own statements in ensuing years that he was not solely responsible for the murders has left a lingering question mark over the case. Indeed, did 'Sam' have more than one 'Son'?

CHAPTER 25

Danny Rolling

Students stalked by knife-wielding campus killer

In 1990, during the first week of classes at the University of Florida, Gainesville, five college students were brutally slain. The crimes sent the community into a panic and it would take nine anxious months before the murderer was publicly named as a suspect.

Danny Harold Rolling, also known as 'The Gainesville Ripper', was born to Claudia and James Rolling in 1954 in Shreveport, Louisiana. His father, a police officer, was abusive and violent to both him, his brother Kevin, and his mother, who made repeated attempts to leave her husband but always returned. He later said of his father: 'Nothing we ever did pleased him. No matter how far we bent over backwards. In the Rolling home you were walking around on eggshells, just so afraid, of what we were going to do to set him off.'

After treatment for schizophrenia and several incarcerations as a teen and young adult for a string of robberies in Georgia, Rolling had trouble trying to assimilate into society and hold down a steady job. In May 1990, he tried to kill his father by shooting him twice during an argument. Thinking he'd succeeded, he fled home leaving a lipsticked message on the mirror: 'I tried. I just can't make it.'

Rolling arrived in Florida, where he began committing petty crimes such as burglary and robbery. He made his home in motels until finally becoming a homeless drifter. Then, at the age of 36, he embarked on one of the most gruesome killing sprees the United States has known.

On 24 August 1990, in the university town of Gainesville, two pretty, brunette students, Christina Powell, 17, and Sonja Larson, 18, were carrying groceries back to their house just before midnight. Unbeknown to them, Rolling, dressed in black and armed with a military knife, automatic weapon and screw-driver, was watching from across the street. After following them home and waiting for their lights to switch off, he prised open their door, crept past Christina, who slept on the couch, and tiptoed upstairs to Sonja's room.

Rolling placed tape across Sonja's mouth to prevent her from screaming. She awoke and fought in vain. The maniac slashed her with his knife again and again, finally killing her. After tossing a blanket over the butchered body, he slipped down-stairs and ripped off another piece of tape to seal the mouth of the still-sleeping Christina. He taped her hands behind her back and then slashed the front of her nightdress.

After savagely raping the trembling girl, he rolled Christina on to her stomach and plunged his knife into her back five times before pouring washing-up liquid over her body in an attempt to destroy any DNA evidence that could positively identify him.

Just one day later, his next victim, Christa Hoyt, 18, met the same grisly end. Rolling had watched her through her bedroom window while she was getting ready for her part-time job at the sheriff's office. While she was at work, he broke into her apartment and waited for her return. Rolling pounced on her from behind the moment she opened the door. Her mouth and hands taped, she was dragged into the bedroom. She too was raped, stabbed and her body sliced from throat to stomach, before being washed in caustic cleanser, leaving a dramatic absence of blood.

After the killer had left the crime scene, he realised he had left his ID card at Christa's apartment. He risked going back for it and, in a sick twist, he rearranged the corpse in such a way as to highlight the carnage in the room. He decapitated Christa Hoyt and set her head on a shelf, surrounding it with carefully positioned mirrors – one set to reflect the grisly scene out to anyone passing by her window and another to catch the look of horror on the face of the first person to discover the body. The headless corpse was seated on the side of the bed so that her arms dangled down by her legs. Inexplicably, a selection of household objects were placed around her.

Two days later, and only hours after the other two girls' bodies were found, Christa's body was discovered after her worried parents, who hadn't heard from her, alerted the police.

The horrific nature of the killings, which involved the mutilation and posing of the victims, shocked the community and sent university students fleeing for home. The town was soon filled with law enforcement officers and reporters from across the nation.

Rolling's next victim was Tracey Paules, 23. Not fleeing town like many of her fellow students, Tracey felt she had little to fear as she shared accommodation with her flatmate, 23-year-old Manuel Taboada, a strapping 6-foot 15-stone football star. However, even Manuel, when caught off guard, was no match for the killer, and despite a brave fight, Rolling stabbed him thirty times.

Hearing the struggle, Tracey woke to find Rolling standing over her flatmate. She ran into her room, locking the door behind her, but Rolling smashed through it, taped Tracey's hands and mouth and raped her before stabbing her to death. He wiped her clean with disinfectant, then washed the blood from himself in her swimming pool outside the apartment block. Tracey's boyfriend alerted the police when she failed to answer his calls the following day.

Police initially had very few leads and, with the terrified townsfolk taking flight while baying for the culprit's blood, enormous pressure was heaped upon them to make an arrest. Several suspects were investigated, including university freshman Edward Humphrey whose fingernail scrapings and hair and blood samples were taken. Edward, 19, had been a handsome athlete and bright student until he developed manic depression. Self-inflicted injuries had left him with a limp and bad facial scarring. Two days before the first murders, Edward had threatened a couple of students who had made fun of him when he'd applied to join their fraternity house. The students reported the incident when the murder rampage continued.

Two days after Tracey and Manuel were killed, Edward, having failed to take his usual medication, attacked his grandmother. When his mother called the police, he was charged with assault – and when a photograph of the crazed student was distributed by police, one woman mistakenly came forward claiming he had raped her. It didn't help that he told police about conversations he'd had with his alter ego, 'John', appearing more and more to fit the profile of the knifeman.

Police had, of course, got the wrong man. And despite Rolling's efforts to destroy DNA evidence at his crime scenes, enough traces of bodily fluids had survived to allow a biological fingerprinting test. Edward's DNA did not match the murderer's and he was released.

With the killer still loose, all the police could do was hunt for the murder weapons and compose a list of items they expected to find in the monster's lair, which included knives, screwdrivers, knickers, bloody shoes, human flesh and nipples.

Yet it was Rolling's reliance on petty crime that led to his eventual capture and murder charges. Ten days after killing Tracey Paules and Manuel Taboada, he robbed a bank with a 9mm pistol and stole a car. The police found the gun the next day at the campsite where he had been hiding out. He had gone on to carry out a series of thefts before he was finally caught in Marion County where he had held up a supermarket.

When police ran a routine check on the small-time thief, a violent past and treatment for schizophrenia were revealed. Not only did the attempted murder of his father come to light but there were similarities between the Gainesville murders and a triple murder in the previous year, 1989, in Rolling's home town. In that case, 24-year-old Julie Grissom had been stripped, murdered and her body posed. Her father William, 55, and 8-year-old son Sean, who had also been in the house, had been killed too. Tape had been used to bind them and their bodies had been cleaned.

The horrific nature of the killings, which involved the mutilation and posing of the victims' bodies, certainly reflected Rolling's macabre signature – but without a confession and little evidence, police could not be certain of a conviction. Nevertheless, in September 1991, he was charged with five counts of murder and was subsequently convicted and sentenced to death by lethal injection.

Rolling appealed his death sentence on a variety of grounds over the next dozen years. His attorney, Baya Harrison, handled his final appeal, arguing the lethal injection procedure was a cruel and unusual punishment. The US Supreme Court's rejection of the appeal paved the way for his execution.

It seemed that prison life had by this time given him plenty of opportunity to ponder his crimes. In a letter to the Associated

Press in 2000, he wrote: 'Any complaint I may have pales in comparison to the terrible wrong I inflicted upon good people. I stand in the shadow of their suffering. If it is to be mercy, then I shall be eternally grateful. If it is to be the wrath of vengeance, then God grant me the strength to face what I must. For I owe a debt I cannot repay ... not even with my own life.'

In a prison interview, he said: 'I could have been a contender. The good Lord gave me some very good talent I could have used in a positive way that could have brought joy to people, and somehow I just fell through the cracks.'

In another, revealing prison interview, referring to his father's abuse, he said: 'I'm not asking for sympathy, but if this can help somebody out there, some parent who is stripping their child of their own identity, their own character at an early age, then they're going to replace that character with something else – and that something else might not be a good thing.'

The 52-year-old serial killer did clear up one loose end before he died. Prior to his execution, he gave a note to his minister confessing to the 1989 triple slaying in Louisiana in which he was suspected but never convicted. He wrote: 'I and I alone am guilty. It was my hand that took those precious lights out of this ole dark world. With all my heart and soul would I could bring them back.'

Rolling was executed by lethal injection on 25 October 2006, and pronounced dead at 6.13pm. He had showed no remorse and had refused to make any comments or offer an apology to the relatives of his victims, several of whom were present at his execution as witnesses.

CHAPTER 26

Angels of Death

Cover-ups and foul-ups hid an epidemic of hospital slayings

There is one kind of serial killer who is not driven by lust or pathological hatred, who does not murder in frenzy, who is unusually cool, calm and – as the forces of law and order worldwide have discovered – is the most elusive of all to convict. These killers are in a venerated position of trust as members of the medical profession. It is almost inconceivable that anyone who devotes his or her life to saving life should turn that ethic on its head and begin instead to take life away. But the proof that it happens is all too clear. The fact that it probably happens far more than we are aware is an eerie afterthought.

There are an alarming and seemingly growing number of nursing staff who have put paid to their vulnerable patients. And sadly, even when alarm bells start ringing, it has often taken literally years for action to be initiated to halt these false 'Angels of Mercy'.

A classic but utterly shameful case is that of Genene Jones, a Texas paediatric nurse whose records were shredded by the hospital where she worked, thereby disguising the true extent of her crimes and the hospital's inaction in tackling them. Jones got a thrill from putting children in mortal peril and thrusting herself into the role of heroine when they pulled through. Sadly, many did not. She is feared to have lethally injected up to forty-seven infants and children in her care over a four-year span in clinics around San Antonio in the early 1980s.

The warning signs had always been there. Born in 1950, Jones was rejected by her real parents and given up for adoption. She remained close to her brother and was distraught when he died young. She was similarly affected when her other brother and father also died of cancer. It was clear that she joined the nursing profession because she 'needed to be needed'. That wasn't easy, because most of her nursing colleagues found her to be a very strange character. She was forced to quit a number of her early nursing positions because of her difficult and sometimes aggressive behaviour. Despite this, she landed a job in the intensive care section of the paediatric unit of Bexar County Medical Center Hospital. There, fellow nurses described her as an attention-seeker, a braggart and someone who could not easily take orders.

Hospital staff found it remarkable that when a baby died, Jones would be grief-stricken as if it were her own child. If allowed, she would sit by the body for hours and insist on taking it to the morgue herself. Despite her peculiar behaviour, she had the support of her head nurse, who liked and protected her. She was subsequently granted authority to oversee the hospital's sickest children, giving her access to a cabinet of medications, of which she made free use.

In 1981, it was noted that an unusual number of babies were dying on her shifts, at one point as many as seven in a fortnight. The infants had been admitted with common childhood symptoms such as fevers, vomiting or diarrhoea but, while in Jones's care, they developed unexplained seizures and suffered cardiac arrest. A typical tiny patient was month-old Rolando Santos, who was being treated for pneumonia but whose unexplained heart problems, extensive haemorrhaging and finally coma all occurred or intensified on Jones's shifts. The baby recovered only when he was placed under 24-hour surveillance.

Fellow staff labelled Jones's on-duty hours 'the Death Shift'. The head of the paediatric unit, Dr James Robotham, made a formal complaint about her after an autopsy on one of the babies in her care revealed traces of Herapin, a drug that causes the heart to stop. Tragically, hospital administrators failed to launch a thorough investigation, fearing the bad publicity for their hospital, and instead simply requested that the drug's use be carefully monitored.

Infant deaths continued but, with Herapin restricted, toxic amounts of another drug, Dilantin, began to arise in laboratory tests. When investigators failed to pin the deaths on just one nurse, a staff restructure was ordered and Jones was moved from the paediatric unit. As a consequence, she resigned.

That should have been the end of Jones's career. Yet in 1982 the killer joined a newly-opened paediatric clinic, in Kerrville, Texas. Within a two-month period, seven children there succumbed to seizures, culminating in the death of a 15-month-old infant, Chelsea Ann McClellan, who had come in for a routine check-up but had been treated by Jones. As with all the other babies who had suffered unexpected seizures, Chelsea had immediately been transferred to Kerr County's Sid Peterson Hospital. Staff there were more alert to the dangers, their suspicions aroused by the sheer volume of children admitted and the fact that, once in their care, the babies speedily recovered. An investigation into the sudden 'epidemic' of infant ailments produced the shock discovery that a similar spate of emergencies had occurred at Bexar County Medical Center Hospital, where Jones had previously worked.

At last the finger of suspicion was pointed at the 'Death Shift' nurse. Chelsea's body was exhumed in October 1982 and it was found that a powerful muscle relaxant, succinylcholine, had been injected. In February 1983, a grand jury was convened in San Antonio to look into a total of forty-seven suspicious deaths of children at Bexar County Medical Center Hospital over a four-year period when Jones had been working there.

It had taken a scandalously inordinate length of time and many unnecessary infant deaths before Jones was finally taken out of circulation. Even then, she was charged only with poisoning one child, Chelsea McClellan, and went on trial for that single murder in January 1984. She was sentenced to ninety-nine years in prison and earned another sixty years in a second trial the same year when she was found guilty of injuring Rolando Santos by injection.

A further scandal was to be revealed during the court cases. Officials at Bexar County Medical Center Hospital had shredded the records of Jones's employment and activities, destroying crucial evidence that was under subpoena. Thus, the 'Death Shift' nurse's final murder count may never be known – though police sources have speculated that Jones may have murdered almost fifty helpless infants since the start of her ill-fated nursing career in 1977.

As can be seen from the case of Genene Jones, it is notoriously difficult to apportion blame for hospital killings.

According to leading forensic scientist Henry Lee, murders by nursing staff are the most difficult serial killings to detect and on which to obtain a conviction. 'You have to figure out who the victims were long after they were buried,' he said. 'Then you have to link them to the suspect. Prepare to fail.'

Lee made his comments after another particularly horrifying case, that of Texas-born Efren Saldivar who, like other nurses similarly accused, became labelled by the media as an 'Angel of Death'. Saldivar confessed to murdering no fewer than fifty patients while working as a respiratory therapist in a Los Angeles hospital.

Saldivar had taken a brief course at North Hollywood medical college in 1988 to qualify for his job at the Glendale Adventist Medical Center, where he worked the night shift, when he was more likely to be able to operate alone. Over a period of ten years, he killed his patients by injecting a paralytic drug which led to respiratory or cardiac arrest.

Police put an end to his silent slaughter in 1998 after authorities, acting on a tip-off from another member of staff found phials of a muscle relaxant in his locker. Then aged 32, he made a full confession, admitting that he had killed his first patient when he was 19 and fresh out of training. The victim, an elderly woman terminally ill with cancer, had been suffering, so Saldivar suffocated her. His next victims died when lethal drugs were fed into their intravenous drips. Much later, in 1997, he became bolder, injecting lethal doses directly into elderly patients. By way of partially excusing his actions, he said he picked only those who were under the standard order: 'Do not resuscitate.' He also said that he had despatched his victims because his department was so understaffed that not all of them could be adequately cared for.

Saldivar's conviction seemed a foregone conclusion until the killer suddenly recanted his confession. To gain adequate evidence against him, twenty of the most recently buried patients had to be exhumed – and six of those bodies contained large amounts of a muscle relaxant drug called Pavulon, which is derived from a South American poison. Presented with the findings, Saldivar confessed all and was brought to court in March 2002, when he pleaded guilty to six counts of murder. His confession allowed him to avoid the death penalty: instead, he was given six consecutive life sentences. The six murders to which he had pleaded guilty were no more than a token charge, however. Even his confession to fifty killings was considered an underestimate, some authorities putting his tally at over 100.

Forensic scientist Henry Lee's comments relating to the Saldivar case – that, by their very nature, it is notoriously difficult to apportion blame for hospital killings – was again proven in the case of a spate of mysterious deaths at a Michigan hospital in 1975. Within just six weeks, no fewer than fifty-six patients died at the Ann Arbor Veterans' Administration Hospital. There were eight deaths on one night alone in only three hours.

The muscle relaxant drug Pavulon, as used two decades later by Efren Saldivar, was revealed as the cause. It was said that large doses had probably been given intravenously, causing patients to cease breathing. The FBI was called in but the deaths of yet another eight patients while investigations were taking place virtually closed the hospital.

Suspicions fell upon two Filipino nurses, 30-year-old Filipina Narcissco and 31-year-old Leonora Perez. Both had always been on duty when the deaths occurred. Despite concerns about another hospital worker who committed suicide in 1976, Narcissco and Perez went on trial the following year charged with eight murders, poisoning and conspiracy. However, the case collapsed when it was revealed that, although patients had stopped dying in large numbers once the nurses had been removed from duty, no one had actually seen them adding anything to the intravenous drips. Perez was discharged on instructions of the judge and Narcissco was found not guilty of murder.

Both nurses were convicted of poisoning and conspiracy, but those convictions were also set aside when an appeal was lodged. Awaiting a retrial, the two women underwent psychiatric testing but were pronounced sane and normal. All charges against them were dismissed at a second trial in February 1978. What exactly happened at the Ann Arbor Veterans' Administration Hospital was to remain a mystery.

Why does an 'Angel of Mercy' become an 'Angel of Death'? In an interview at the Warren Correctional Institution in Lebanon, Ohio, in 1991, former male nurse Donald Harvey, serving several life sentences for murdering dozens of his patients, said: 'People controlled me for eighteen years, and then I controlled my own destiny. I controlled other people's lives, whether they lived or died. I had that power to control. After I didn't get caught for the first fifteen, I thought it was my right. I appointed myself judge, prosecutor and jury. So I played God.'

How Harvey ever got a job working in hospitals is in itself a condemnation of the system. Born in 1952 and raised in the Appalachian Mountains, he was a shy homosexual who dabbled in the occult but was also obsessed with all things medical. At the age of 18, he took a part-time post as a junior orderly at Marymount Hospital in London, Kentucky, where, he was later to confess, he killed twelve patients in ten months by suffocation or removing their oxygen supply. His reason: 'I wanted to ease their suffering.'

At the age of 20, Harvey joined the US Air Force but was discharged less than a year later and was committed with mental disorders to the Veterans' Administration Medical Center in Lexington. The state of his health does not seem to have been improved by attempts to treat him by the application of electroshock therapy. Upon his discharge from hospital, Harvey disguised his recent medical history and got part-time jobs as a nursing assistant and as a clerk at three Kentucky hospitals, before moving to Ohio in 1975 to work at the Cincinnati Veterans' Association Medical Center in jobs that included nursing aide, laboratory technician and mortuary assistant. There, he literally got away with murder for ten years.

How easy it was to avoid detection or conviction was proved when a routine search by security guards in 1985 revealed on Harvey's person an array of hypodermic needles, cocaine-snorting equipment and a .38 calibre pistol. He was fired – but went straight into the next job, as a nursing aide at Cincinnati's Drake Memorial Hospital.

Harvey must have felt invulnerable. He began killing his patients in ever increasing numbers by poisoning them with arsenic, cyanide, insulin, morphine or fluid tainted with hepatitis B and/or HIV. He would also sprinkle rat poison on their food, inject air into their veins, stab them with a coat hanger pushed through a catheter, disconnect their life support machines or suffocate them with plastic bags and wet towels.

Harvey kept a diary of his crimes, which eventually helped convict him. But even though his colleagues openly referred to him as the 'Angel of Death', it took an autopsy on one of his victims in 1987 to reveal him as a poisoner. The diary catalogued his killings: fifteen patients in ten years at the Cincinnati Veterans' Association Medical Center, twenty-three in thirteen months at Drake Memorial. Not all his victims were elderly patients. After a lovers' tiff, he tried to poison his gay partner Carl Heeler, who ended up in hospital but survived. He also administered poison to Heeler's mother and father; she survived but he was admitted to hospital – where Harvey laced his food and where he died in May 1983.

When he was finally arrested, Harvey feigned insanity, at first confessing to thirty-three murders, then fifty, then eighty-plus. His mental state made it difficult to sift fact from fiction, though the Cincinnati prosecutor's office was clear in its assertion when Harvey was brought to court in August 1987 that 'this man is sane and competent but is a compulsive killer'. In three separate trials, in Ohio and Kentucky, he was convicted of forty murders and was given fifteen life terms in prison. The true tally of his murders, however, may never be known.

It may appear from these cases that the 'Angels of Death' syndrome is a particularly American trait. Two classic cases show this not to be the case – the better-known being that of Beverley Allitt, a plain, overweight, frumpy English girl of whom nobody in the Lincolnshire town of Corby Glen took much notice but who was always relied on to be sensible, caring and diligent.

Allitt reputedly suffered from Munchausen's Disease by Proxy, a rare disorder which produces phantom ailments and, in extreme cases, can cause sufferers to harm others deliberately so that they can 'make them better' later. At 17, Allitt took a nursing course which qualified her for her first job: as a trainee nurse at the local Grantham and Kesteven General Hospital. She was placed on the paediatric ward – the most dangerous place anyone with Munchausen's could possibly be.

It was this undiscovered syndrome which led Allitt to become a hospital serial killer. In May 1993, she also entered criminal history as the worst British female serial killer of modern times when she was found guilty at Nottingham Crown Court of murdering four children and attacking nine others. All had been on Ward 4 of the hospital.

Her first victim, a 7-week-old boy, died of a massive heart attack in February 1991, just two days after being admitted with a chest infection. A mentally and physically handicapped 11-year-old boy was killed within three hours of being admitted following an epileptic fit. A 2-month-old girl died after suffering convulsions at home hours after being released from hospital following an insulin overdose. Allitt's last victim, 15-month-old Claire Peck, died on 22 April after being admitted with asthma.

Police were called in only after Claire's death, although nine other children's conditions had become dramatically life-threatening during the period. But once blood tests had been carried out on other victims, a simple check of staff rotas showed that the common factor was Beverley Allitt. She had administered to the children lethal and near-lethal overdoses of both insulin and potassium chloride. She had also tried to suffocate some of them.

At her trial, Allitt's twisted logic became apparent; she believed she was doing no wrong in killing without mercy. The 24-year-old nurse showed no emotion as she was given four life sentences.

The undue delays in the authorities waking up to the fact that they have a killer in their midst is also apparent in the extraordinary case of a string of hospital killings in Austria, which that country's Chancellor, Franz Vranitzky, described in 1991 as 'the most brutal and gruesome crime in our nation's history'.

The perpetrators – for, extraordinarily, there was more than a single killer – were only unmasked when a group of nursing aides at Vienna's Lainz General Hospital, which specialised in geriatric cases, were overheard laughing and joking in a bar about speeding the death of one of their patients. A horrified doctor at an adjoining table reported the conversation to police and an investigation was launched that, at one stage, put the total body count at an astonishing 300 elderly people.

The group's ringleader, Waltraud Wagner, had been 23 when, in 1983, she claimed her first victim, disposing of a patient with an overdose of morphine. She later recruited into this unusual criminal gang three other members of the hospital nursing staff: Maria Gruber, 19, Irene Leidolf, 21, and Stephanija Mayer, 43.

These 'Angels of Death', who usually worked the night shift, devised their own method of murder. One would hold the elderly victim's head and nose, while another would pour water into the person's mouth, causing drowning. The attacks went undetected because elderly patients were frequently found to have fluid in their lungs.

The killings went on for six years, until their loud voices during the 1989 bar-room drinking session gave them away. Under arrest, Wagner confessed to causing thirty-nine deaths – a total she later reduced to only ten cases of 'mercy killing'. She said: 'The ones who got on my nerves were despatched to a free bed with the good Lord. They sometimes resisted but we were stronger. We could decide whether the old fools lived or died. Their ticket to God was long overdue anyway.'

In March 1991, she was sentenced to life for fifteen murders and seventeen attempted murders. Irene Leidolf got a life sentence for five murders, Stephanija Mayer fifteen years for manslaughter and seven attempted murders, and Maria Gruber fifteen years for two attempted murders. When the case was closed, the body count officially stood at forty-two, but many put the final tally at between 200 and 300 victims.

CHAPTER 27

Doctors of Death

Britain's most prolific serial killer left 24-year trail of corpses

If the notion of a nurse turning from life-saving to life-taking (previous chapter) is anathema, then the rare instances of a doctor doing so are an even greater abhorrence. Uniquely trusted, with adherence to a supposedly watertight ethical code, they are normally above suspicion. Yet the two cases instanced below prove that, when we are not watchful, evil can come even in the guise of a member of the medical profession.

Indeed, in the entire annals of British criminal history, it was a doctor, Harold Shipman, whose twenty-four-year-long trail of corpses made him the country's most prolific serial killer. And if the more dramatic estimates for the number of victims of America's Michael Swango were ever able to be proven, they would make him the most prolific serial killer ever.

Dr Harold Shipman took his own life in Wakefield Prison, Yorkshire, on 13 January 2004. The official announcement read: 'Mr Shipman was found hanging in his cell at 6.20am and, despite the best efforts of staff who immediately attempted resuscitation, he was pronounced dead by a doctor at 8.10am. Since arriving at Wakefield on 18 June 2003, Shipman had never been on a suicide watch.'

Families of his victims found it ironic that such strenuous efforts had been made to revive a doctor who had failed to keep alive at least 215 patients entrusted to his care.

Harold Frederick Shipman was born on 14 January 1946, one of eight children of a loving mother to whom he was devoted. It was due to her encouragement that he won a place at grammar school, and when she died at only 43, he became, psychiatrists later testified, 'permanently traumatised and resentful'. At school and later at medical college, Shipman was said to have felt inadequate when in the company of girls. However, at the age of 20, he struck up a conversation on a local bus with 17-year-old Primrose Mary Oxtoby, a farmworker's daughter who worked as a trainee window-dresser for a Leeds department store. When Primrose discovered she was pregnant, the couple married in November 1966, and they went on to have four children: a girl and three boys.

Shipman graduated from Leeds School of Medicine in 1970 when he was aged 24. His first post was in a hospital at Pontefract, West Yorkshire, after which he joined a local general practice in Todmorden. In 1975, he was caught forging prescriptions and stealing drugs for his own use. In court, he pleaded guilty and asked for seventy-four other offences to be taken into consideration. He was fined £600, sent briefly to a drug rehabilitation clinic and emerged supposedly rehabilitated – and ready to accept a temporary position conducting baby clinics in County Durham. There, he was supervised throughout because of his past record.

By the end of 1977, Shipman was considered to have sufficiently rehabilitated himself to be allowed back into general practice and moved to Hyde, Greater Manchester, where he worked as a GP at the Donneybrook Medical Centre through the 1980s before, in 1993, founding his own surgery on the town's Market Street. To the people of Hyde, Shipman was a respected member of the community. To them, his old conviction was not known about; to the authorities it was long forgotten. As for his colleagues, they remained blissfully unaware, since their professional body, the General Medical Council, had never called Shipman to face disciplinary action but had simply written him a letter warning him against future misconduct.

Although suspected, it is not known whether Shipman killed anyone before arriving at Hyde, where his colleagues at the Donneybrook surgery felt he was bossy and arrogant but where his patients saw only a kindly, confident general practitioner. His first known victim once he arrived in Hyde was 76-year-old Mary Winterbottom, retired stewardess of her local Conservative Club, who died on 21 September 1984, who was visited at home by Shipman after complaining of a persistent cold. The doctor said he had simply found the old lady 'lying dead on her bed'.

Three months later, the GP claimed his next known victim, Eileen Cox, a 72-year-old retired hairdresser, who died at home 'following a heart attack'. May Brooks, aged 74, a civil engineer's widow, died in her chair at home in February 1985 following a routine visit by Shipman. Jewellery was subsequently found to be missing. Two weeks later, 89-year-old widow Margaret Conway died at home 'from a stroke'.

Suspicious deaths continued at the average rate of one a year until Shipman left the Hyde group practice and founded his own surgery in 1993. Then the number of deaths escalated – eight that year, starting with a 92-year-old who was found dead within hours of a visit by her GP. Shipman claimed at least six victims in 1994, ten in 1995, sixteen in 1996, twenty-two in 1997 and ten in 1998.

It was not astute detection by police that brought Shipman's killing spree to a close. It was the intervention in March 1998 of a 28-year-old local undertaker, Deborah Massey. She voiced her concern that, in her words, 'there were just too many deaths for a one-doctor surgery'. A coroner was alerted and he called in Greater Manchester Police. Even then, action was not taken swiftly enough to save three more doomed patients before Shipman was finally arrested.

Before that happened, the daughter of one of his last victims also alerted the police. Her mother, former Mayor Kathleen Grundy, a seemingly healthy 81-year-old, had been found dead at her home in June 1998, Shipman giving the cause of death as 'old age'. Only afterwards was it discovered that the old lady had left her entire £386,000 estate to the doctor – her will having been typed on Shipman's own typewriter and with his fingerprints all over it. Mrs Grundy's body was exhumed and lethal levels of morphine were found: Shipman said Mrs Grundy was a drug addict and showed police hand-written case notes to back this up. They were clearly false. Police quickly established that he had backdated them to a day when he had been away on holiday.

Shipman, by then a 52-year-old married father of four, was arrested in September and brought to court in Preston on 12 October 1999, when he denied one charge of forging Mrs

Grundy's will and fifteen charges of murder. 'All of them died most unexpectedly,' said the prosecuting counsel, Richard Henriques, QC, 'and all of them had seen Dr Shipman on the day of their death.' He added that Shipman's drive to kill was fed by a God-like belief that he had power over life and death.

'There is no question of euthanasia or what is sometimes called mercy-killing. None of the deceased were terminally ill. The defendant killed those fifteen patients because he enjoyed doing so. He was exercising the ultimate power of controlling life and death and repeated it so often that he must have found the drama of taking life to his taste.' Mr Henriques said that tests carried out on the thigh muscle of each of the deceased established a significant presence of morphine within the bodies.

During the four-month trial, the catalogue of his killings was avidly listened to by the Shipmans' children: Sarah, 32, Christopher, 28, David, 20, and 17-year-old Samuel. Their mother Primrose also sat in court, showing no emotion. They heard how Shipman regularly administered lethal heroin injections, all the while telling his patients that he was giving them something to ease their breathing or make them feel better. He generally signed the death certificates as 'natural causes' and advised relatives not to seek a post mortem because 'it will only add to your grief'.

The jury deliberated for six days before reaching unanimous verdicts. Even when a jubilant cry of 'Yes!' rang out from one of the deceaseds' relatives as the first verdict was announced, neither Shipman nor wife Primrose displayed any emotion.

The judge, Mr Justice Forbes, then told the murderous doctor: 'These were wicked, wicked, crimes. Each of your victims was your patient. You murdered each and every one of your victims by a calculating and cold-blooded perversion of your medical skills. For your own evil and wicked purpose, you took advantage and grossly abused the trust each of your victims put in you. I have little doubt each of your victims smiled and thanked you as she submitted to your deadly administrations. None of your victims realised that yours was not a healing touch.'

When the judge told Shipman he was going to prison for life, his wife Primrose still did not reveal her feelings. Since then, she has spoken only once about her husband, and that was to maintain his innocence at one of the subsequent inquiries into the deaths. The investigations were ordered because of the extraordinary series of blunders that allowed Shipman to carry on killing. It emerged that detectives had investigated him six months before he was finally caught, following concerns about the number of elderly women dying unexpectedly in their homes. The death rate among female patients over 65 was three times the national average but a police inquiry failed to spot anything sinister. There was not even a check that would have revealed Shipman's previous record for his dishonesty and drug addiction.

During his time as a GP at Hyde, Shipman obtained huge amounts of heroin-based drugs by writing out prescriptions in the name of patients and telling the pharmacy next to his surgery that he would deliver them himself. At one stage, Shipman obtained 12,000mg of diamorphine, enough to kill about 350 people.

Psychiatrists who examined the doctor after he began his prison sentence issued this report to one inquiry into the murders: 'He could only get what he wanted by killing elderly women. He did it to make himself feel better. But his focus was on the act of killing and it was important to him to be in control of the process. In some ways you can view him as a necrophile because he needed bodies. But he had no interest in them after death. It was the killing – the point of death – that interested him. Dr Shipman is a fairly extreme example of a control freak. In his mind, the killings would have been outside the normal moral framework, so he would not feel any remorse.'

It was not until January 2002, two years after his trial, that Shipman was confirmed as Britain's biggest-ever serial killer with an official toll of 215 victims. The figure was the result of an inquiry headed by High Court judge Dame Janet Smith into the deaths of 887 patients in Shipman's care. Of his 215 confirmed victims, 171 were women and 44 were men. Nearly all were elderly and living alone. In her report, titled 'Death Disguised', Dame Janet said: 'Deeply shocking though it is, the bare statement that Shipman has killed over 200 patients does not fully reflect the enormity of his crimes. As a general practitioner, he was trusted implicitly by his patients and their families. He betrayed that trust in a way and to an extent that I believe is unparalleled in history. The way in which Shipman could kill, face relatives and walk away unsuspected would have been dismissed as fanciful if it had been described in a work of fiction. He disguised his character and the true nature of his victims so as to deceive, not only his victims and their families, but also his professional colleagues and those responsible for death registration and cremation certificate procedures.'

Shipman was jailed in top-security prisons and told he would never be released. He carried out his own death sentence, using bedsheets tied to his window bars. He was found hanged in his cell at Wakefield Prison, at 6.20am on 13 January 2004, which was the eve of his 58th birthday. The manifest opprobrium in which he was held by the British public was summed up by a headline in the tabloid newspaper *The Sun* which exulted: 'Ship Ship hooray!'

By contrast, American medical murderer Michael Swango was only ever convicted of four murders – yet he is believed to have killed between thirty-five and sixty patients in the United States and perhaps hundreds more overseas. Following his trial and conviction in 2000, the university where he trained issued this sombre appraisal: 'If Swango is legally connected to all the suspicious deaths of patients under his care since he began (his medical career) in 1983, it would make him the most prolific serial killer in history.'

In echoes of the Harold Shipman case, Swango had been able to kill with impunity as the authorities turned a blind eye to danger signs that, in hindsight, seem too obvious to miss. He took up doctoring positions at hospitals across two continents without anyone checking on the trail of death he had left behind him. He poisoned patients in New York State, South Dakota, Illinois and Ohio as well as in Zambia and Namibia in Africa.

Born Michael Joseph Swango in Tacoma, Washington State, on 21 October 1954, he did well at school, studying music and then biology. He was also an enthusiastic member of the Christian Brothers High School Marching Band. However, his other obsessive interests were with war and violence, donning military fatigues and keeping a scrapbook of cuttings on air and car crashes, riots and sex crimes. When challenged by his mother over his morbid interest, he replied: 'If I'm ever accused of murder, this will prove I'm mentally unstable.'

After a short spell in the US Marine Corps, he worked as an ambulance attendant, a job he later said he enjoyed because he got to see the blood, injuries and twisted metal of car crashes. Finally, he enrolled at Southern Illinois University to study medicine. Here, some further clues to his character became all too apparent. Fellow medical students described him as 'totally nuts'. He would fabricate patient reports. If chided for making a mistake, Swango would drop to the floor and perform punishing push-ups. He would make light of patients' dying moments, one of his catchphrases being: 'Hey, death happens.'

After an enforced extra year's study, Swango graduated in medicine in 1983, at the age of 28, winning a year-long internship in general surgery at the Ohio State University Medical Center. In January 1984, it was first noted that the newcomer was acting suspiciously, appearing on wards at times when he was due to be off-duty. A nurse saw him checking on a patient to whom he had recently been attending and found the woman turning blue from respiratory failure. Emergency treatment saved her but a week later she was again found gasping for air and soon afterwards suffocated. Swango had been the last person to attend to her.

The next day, another elderly woman, recovering after an operation, was found blue and shaking shortly after Swango had left her room. Resuscitated, she asked for a pencil and notebook and wrote: 'Someone gave me some med in my IV (intravenous drip) and paralysed all of me – lungs, heart, speech.' When anxious nurses compared notes, they discovered that at least six other patients, all evidently making good progress, had suddenly died. Their ages ranged from a 19-year-old to a 47-year-old. In each case, Swango had been the duty intern.

An investigation was ordered but it was slipshod. Incredibly, none of the nurses who had raised the alarm were interviewed. If they had been, their comments would have reflected the reasons for the doctor being nicknamed 'Double-O Swango'– a reference to 007 James Bond's 'license to kill'. Without their evidence being heeded, however, the high number of deaths whenever Swango was around continued. He shocked one grieving relative by telling her bluntly: 'Your mother's dead now. You can go look at her.' Complaints about Swango were at last heard by the administrators, however, and the hospital terminated the killer's contract of employment.

Swango returned to his home town of Quincy, Illinois, where he joined the Adams County Ambulance Corps. His fellow ambulance crew members found him decidedly odd. In an off-duty moment, he once related to them his favourite fantasy: 'Picture a school bus crammed with kids smashing head-on with a trailer truck loaded down with gasoline. We're summoned. We get there in a jiffy just as another gasoline truck rams the bus. Up in flames it goes. Kids are hurled through the air, everywhere, on telephone poles, on the street, especially along an old barbed wire fence along the road. All burning.'

On one occasion, an entire paramedic crew became ill after eating doughnuts brought in by Swango. His colleagues decided to investigate the newcomer a little further – and found arsenic in his locker. When alerted, police searched the poisoner's apartment and discovered a hoard of phials, bottles, syringes and a library of books on murder. There was also a selection of guns and knives.

Swango was arrested and charged with seven counts of aggravated battery. The press dubbed him the 'Doughnut Poisoner' when he appeared in court in April 1985 and was sentenced to five years' imprisonment. Judge Dennis Cashman told him: 'It is clearly obvious to me that every man, woman and child in this community or anywhere else you might go is in jeopardy as long as you are a free person. You deserve the maximum under the law because there is no excuse for what you have done.'

The judge's advice was not heeded. Two years later, Swango was released for good behaviour. Wisely, his application for a medical licence in the state of Virginia was turned down and, happily for hospital staff and patients, he spent the next few years in various jobs away from medicine. He also had a girl-friend, Kirstin Kinney, a 26-year-old nurse who moved with him to South Dakota in 1992 when Swango accepted a position as emergency doctor at the Veterans Affairs Medical Center in Sioux Falls. Both Kirstin and Swango made their mark in their new jobs, he being regarded as one of the best emergency doctors the hospital had ever known, and she as one of the most dedicated nurses at the local Royal C. Johnson Veterans Memorial Hospital.

Both their love affair and their careers came to a sudden halt, however, when a programme about the notorious 'Doughnut Poisoner' was shown on television. Swango was dismissed but a farewell party was thrown for him by a group of loyal friends. All the guests fell ill with food-poisoning symptoms. Kirstin now became wise to her partner's evil ways. Realising that the migraine headaches she suffered seemed to disappear whenever she was away from her boyfriend, she fled home, penned a note to her parents and shot herself. Perhaps Swango's most tragic victim, she wrote: 'I love you both. I just didn't want to be here anymore. Just found day-to-day living a constant struggle with my thoughts. I'd say I'm sorry but I'm not. I feel that sense of peace, the peace of mind that I've been looking for. It's nice.' In a second note, left for Swango, she wrote: 'I love you more! You're the most precious man I've ever known.'

It was not good police work or the vigilance of hospital authorities that finally halted Swango but Kirstin Kinney's parents, who could not forgive him for driving their daughter to suicide. After their daughter's death, Swango had moved to New York State where, with the fake references he had become expert in forging, in 1993 he got a job at the Veterans Administration Headquarters, Northport, Long Island. His first patient died within hours of his arrival. Others were also to die in his 'care', all suffering heart failure in the dead of night. The wife of one of his victims even sued the hospital after seeing Swango inject a liquid into her husband's neck, but the case was thrown out due to lack of evidence.

Kirstin Kinney's parents were more persistent. Appalled that Swango was still practising, they alerted the Long Island hospital and he was sacked, the hospital authorities writing to every medical school in America warning them about him.

Swango disappeared, surfacing again in Africa. More forged documents secured him jobs in Zimbabwe in 1995, first in the operating theatres of Mpilo Hospital, Bulawayo, and then at the Mnene Lutheran Outpost Hospital, where patients started to die with alarming regularity. A police investigation was launched and Swango fled to neighbouring Zambia, then to

Europe, and finally back to America. He was arrested the moment he landed at Chicago's O'Hare Airport in June 1997.

While languishing in jail, psychologists examined Swango and diagnosed him as a psychopath with a 'preoccupation to control and manipulate'. One said: 'One of the most chilling things about this kind of personality is that there is no known treatment, no psychiatric procedure, no drug, no way to stop him. If he is free, he will find a means and a place to do it again.'

Swango was finally charged with four counts of murder, pleaded guilty and, in July 2000, was sentenced to life imprisonment without parole. He was later given another life sentence for the murder of Cynthia McGee after the discovery of a diary in which he had written about her killing: 'I love the sweet, husky, close smell of indoor homicide. Murdering is the only way I have of reminding myself I am still alive.'

Although only ever convicted of four murders, Swango was suspected of many more, estimates that included his overseas work ranging into the hundreds. As an FBI agent said at the time of his conviction: 'We believe that in the States alone, Swango can be linked to 100 or more mysterious deaths of patients directly in his care. It is a national scandal.'